**Contributing Editor**
Sara Connolly

**Editor in Chief**
Karen J. Goldfluss, M.S. Ed.

**Creative Director**
Sarah M. Fournier

**Cover Artist**
Sarah Kim

**Imaging**
Leonard P. Swierski

**Publisher**
Mary D. Smith, M.S. Ed.

For correlations to the Common Core State Standards, see page 105 of this book or visit *http://www.teachercreated.com/standards/*.

**Teacher Created Resources**

12621 Western Avenue
Garden Grove, CA 92841
www.teachercreated.com

ISBN: 978-1-4206-8085-0

*© 2017 Teacher Created Resources*
Made in U.S.A.

# Table of Contents

# Introduction

The *Minutes to Mastery* series was designed to help students build confidence in their math abilities, and then bring that confidence into testing situations. As students develop fluency with math facts and operations, they improve their abilities to do different types of math problems comfortably and quickly.

Each of the 100 tests in the book has 10 questions in key math areas. Multiple opportunities are presented to solve the standards-based problems and develop speed and fluency. The pages present problems in a variety of ways using different terminology. For example, students might be asked to divide and then later asked to find an equal share. Multiple terms are used to provide additional practice in decoding text for clues. Critical thinking and abstract reasoning play an important role in solving math problems, and practicing skills is imperative.

Keep in mind that timing can sometimes add to the stress of learning. If this is the experience for your math learner(s), focus less on timing in the beginning. As confidence builds, accuracy and speed will follow. Timing can be introduced later.

Following are steps to help you establish a timing system.

1. Allow students to complete a worksheet without officially timing it to get a sense of how long it will take them to complete it. Ideally, you want all ten questions per page to be answered.

2. Remind students to write their answers legibly.

3. Allow students to practice using the preferred amount of time before taking a timed test.

4. Have students take a few timed tests and see how it works. Adjust the time as needed.

5. Work to improve the number of correct answers within the given time. Remind students that it is important to be accurate—not just fast!

6. Encourage students to try to do their best each time, to review their results, and to spend time working on areas where they had difficulties.

The section at the bottom of each page can be used to record specific progress on that test, including the time the student started the test, finished the test, the total time taken, how many problems were completed, and how many problems were correct.

A tracking sheet is provided on page 4 of this book. Use the second column to record the number of problems students answered correctly, and the final column to record the score as a percent, the date the test was taken, initials, or anything else that helps you and your students to keep track of their progress.

With practice, all students can begin to challenge themselves to increase their speed while completing problems clearly and accurately.

# Tracking Sheet

Name _____

| Numbers, Adding, and Subtracting | | |
|---|---|---|
| Test 1 | /10 | |
| Test 2 | /10 | |
| Test 3 | /10 | |
| Test 4 | /10 | |
| Test 5 | /10 | |
| Test 6 | /10 | |
| Test 7 | /10 | |
| Test 8 | /10 | |
| Test 9 | /10 | |
| Test 10 | /10 | |
| Test 11 | /10 | |
| Test 12 | /10 | |
| Multiplication and Division | | |
| Test 13 | /10 | |
| Test 14 | /10 | |
| Test 15 | /10 | |
| Test 16 | /10 | |
| Test 17 | /10 | |
| Test 18 | /10 | |
| Test 19 | /10 | |
| Test 20 | /10 | |
| Test 21 | /10 | |
| Fractions | | |
| Test 22 | /10 | |
| Test 23 | /10 | |
| Test 24 | /10 | |
| Test 25 | /10 | |
| Test 26 | /10 | |
| Test 27 | /10 | |
| Test 28 | /10 | |
| Test 29 | /10 | |
| Test 30 | /10 | |
| Test 31 | /10 | |
| Decimals | | |
| Test 32 | /10 | |
| Test 33 | /10 | |
| Test 34 | /10 | |
| Test 35 | /10 | |
| Test 36 | /10 | |
| Test 37 | /10 | |
| Test 38 | /10 | |

| | | |
|---|---|---|
| Test 39 | /10 | |
| Test 40 | /10 | |
| Test 41 | /10 | |
| Test 42 | /10 | |
| Test 43 | /10 | |
| Percentages | | |
| Test 44 | /10 | |
| Test 45 | /10 | |
| Test 46 | /10 | |
| Test 47 | /10 | |
| Order of Operations and Mixed Operations | | |
| Test 48 | /10 | |
| Test 49 | /10 | |
| Test 50 | /10 | |
| Test 51 | /10 | |
| Test 52 | /10 | |
| Test 53 | /10 | |
| Test 54 | /10 | |
| Test 55 | /10 | |
| Test 56 | /10 | |
| Test 57 | /10 | |
| Geometry | | |
| Test 58 | /10 | |
| Test 59 | /10 | |
| Test 60 | /10 | |
| Test 61 | /10 | |
| Test 62 | /10 | |
| Test 63 | /10 | |
| Test 64 | /10 | |
| Test 65 | /10 | |
| Test 66 | /10 | |
| Test 67 | /10 | |
| Test 68 | /10 | |
| Test 69 | /10 | |
| Test 70 | /10 | |
| Time | | |
| Test 71 | /10 | |
| Test 72 | /10 | |
| Test 73 | /10 | |
| Test 74 | /10 | |
| Test 75 | /10 | |
| Test 76 | /10 | |

| Probability and Statistics | | |
|---|---|---|
| Test 77 | /10 | |
| Test 78 | /10 | |
| Test 79 | /10 | |
| Test 80 | /10 | |
| Test 81 | /10 | |
| Test 82 | /10 | |
| Test 83 | /10 | |
| Test 84 | /10 | |
| Test 85 | /10 | |
| Test 86 | /10 | |
| Test 87 | /10 | |
| Test 88 | /10 | |
| Test 89 | /10 | |
| Test 90 | /10 | |
| Equations and Variables | | |
| Test 91 | /10 | |
| Test 92 | /10 | |
| Test 93 | /10 | |
| Test 94 | /10 | |
| Test 95 | /10 | |
| Test 96 | /10 | |
| Test 97 | /10 | |
| Test 98 | /10 | |
| Test 99 | /10 | |
| Test 100 | /10 | |

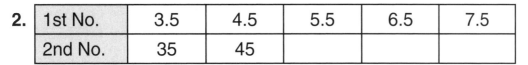

Name _____    Date _____

## Complete each of the following tables and identify the rule that you used.

**1.**

| 1st No. | 4 | 5 | 6 | 7 | 8 |
|---|---|---|---|---|---|
| 2nd No. | 24 | 30 | 36 | | |

Rule: _____

**2.**

| 1st No. | 3.5 | 4.5 | 5.5 | 6.5 | 7.5 |
|---|---|---|---|---|---|
| 2nd No. | 35 | 45 | | | |

Rule: _____

**3.**

| 1st No. | 63 | 72 | 81 | 90 | 99 |
|---|---|---|---|---|---|
| 2nd No. | | 8 | | | 11 |

Rule: _____

**4.**

| 1st No. | 1 | 2 | 3 | 4 | 5 |
|---|---|---|---|---|---|
| 2nd No. | 1/2 | | | | 2 1/2 |

Rule: _____

## Continue each of the following number patterns.

**5.** 9, 10, 12, 15, _____, _____, _____

**6.** 104, 93, 83, 74, _____, _____, _____

**7.** 2, 2.5, 3.5, 5, _____, _____, _____

**8.** 4, 7, 12, 19, _____, _____, _____

## Apply the rule to complete each pattern.

**9.** $2 \times \blacksquare + 5 = \star$

| $\blacksquare$ | 2 | 4 | 6 | 8 | 10 |
|---|---|---|---|---|---|
| $\star$ | | | | | |

**10.** $3 \times \blacksquare - 6 = \star$

| $\blacksquare$ | 5 | 6 | 7 | 8 | 9 |
|---|---|---|---|---|---|
| $\star$ | | | | | |

| Started: | Finished: | Total Time: | Completed: | Correct: |
|---|---|---|---|---|

Name _____    Date _____

## Add the following.

**1.**   568,291
        367,681
    + 107,303

**2.**   872,456
        619,562
    + 116,721

**3.**   548,312
        234,801
    +  23,427

## Find the total of:

**4.** $369,452 and $647,189 _____

**5.** $157,261 and $823,481 _____

**6.** $632,876 and $321,424 _____

## Find the total measurements. Include the units in your answer.

**7.**    8,621 feet
         6,972
     + 11,875

**8.**    6,693 pounds
         9,854
     +  3,697

## Add the following.

**9.**    328,249.6
      +  925,258.8

## Rewrite the answer to problem 9 in words.

**10.** _____

_____

_____

| Started: | Finished: | Total Time: | Completed: | Correct: |
|----------|-----------|-------------|------------|----------|

Name _____ Date _____

**Round each of the following to the nearest hundred.**

    **1.** 867 _____

    **2.** 424 _____

**Round each of the following to the nearest thousand.**

    **3.** 984 _____

    **4.** 3,293 _____

**Estimate an answer for each of the following by first rounding each number to the nearest thousand.**

|     | Problem | Rounded | Estimate |
| --- | --- | --- | --- |
| **5.** | 6,429 + 2,374 | | |
| **6.** | 5,238 + 6,207 | | |
| **7.** | 36,207 + 10,291 | | |

**True or false? To the nearest ten,**

    **8.** 923 rounds to 930. _____

    **9.** 855 rounds to 850. _____

    **10.** 648 rounds to 650. _____

| Started: | Finished: | Total Time: | Completed: | Correct: |
| --- | --- | --- | --- | --- |

Name _____    Date _____

## Subtract the following.

1.   96,425
    – 18,257

2.   29,400
    –  6,231

3.   69,248
    – 51,580

## Estimate the answer to each problem by first rounding each number to the nearest thousand. Rewrite and solve the estimated problem in the space beside the original problem.

4.   56,287
    – 36,284

5.   87,695
    – 22,104

## Subtract the following measurements. Include the units in your answer.

6.   624,891 inches
    – 321,963

7.   958,452 feet
    – 612,258

8.   657,125 yards
    – 210,698

9.   925,845 miles
    – 690,650

## Solve the following word problem.

10. The profit from Saturday's concert was $562,497. The profit from Sunday's concert was $384,165. How much more of a profit was made at Saturday's concert? _____

| Started: | Finished: | Total Time: | Completed: | Correct: |
|---|---|---|---|---|

8

Name _____    Date _____

## Subtract the following.

1.  5,328,021
   − 2,254,101

2.  6,987,305
   −  940,456

## The area of eight states (including water) is given below in square miles.

| Alaska (AK) | California (CA) | Delaware (DE) | Florida (FL) |
|---|---|---|---|
| 663,267 mi.$^2$ | 163,695 mi.$^2$ | 2,489 mi.$^2$ | 65,755 mi.$^2$ |
| Hawaii (HI) | Nevada (NV) | Oregon (OR) | Texas (TX) |
| 10,931 mi.$^2$ | 110,560 mi.$^2$ | 98,380 mi.$^2$ | 268,580 mi.$^2$ |

## Find the difference in area between:

3. AK and TX _____

4. OR and HI _____

5. NV and DE _____

6. CA and FL _____

7. TX and NV _____

8. AK and HI _____

## Subtract the following amounts:

9.  $3,258,927
  − $1,498,200

10.  $11,014,207
   −  $360,654

| Started: | Finished: | Total Time: | Completed: | Correct: |
|---|---|---|---|---|

Name _____ Date _____

**Estimate each sum by first rounding each number to the nearest hundred. Rewrite and solve the estimated problem in the space beside the original problem.**

**1.**   25,697
      + 29,208

**2.**   42,392
      + 10,421

**3.**   278,325
      + 308,927

**4.**   104,620
      + 307,922

**Estimate each difference by first rounding each number to the nearest thousand. Rewrite and solve the estimated problem in the space beside the original problem.**

**5.**   46,525
      – 18,949

**6.**   32,250
      –  9,627

**7.**   256,201
      – 125,429

**8.**   801,429
      – 622,780

**Estimate each answer by first rounding each amount to the nearest dollar.**

**9.** $625.95 + $42.45 _____

**10.** $884.32 – $366.89 _____

| Started: | Finished: | Total Time: | Completed: | Correct: |
|---|---|---|---|---|

Name _____    Date _____

**Write *true* or *false* for each of the following.**

**1.** $36 - \bigstar + 5 = 27$     $\bigstar = 4$ _____

**2.** $100 \div \bigstar \times 3 = 30$     $\bigstar = 10$ _____

**3.** $25 - \bigstar = 14.3$     $\bigstar = 10.7$ _____

**4.** $(60 \times \bigstar) \times \frac{1}{3} = 300$     $\bigstar = 10$ _____

**Find the value of the missing numbers.**

**5.** $7 \times \boxed{\phantom{0}} = 40 - 12$

**6.** $18 \div 3 = 5 + \boxed{\phantom{0}}$

**7.** $300 \div 15 = 16 + \boxed{\phantom{0}}$

**Check if each of the following word problems is correct. If it is correct, write *true*. If it is incorrect, write *false* and then correct it.**

**8.** 64 carrots were shared among 8 horses. Each horse received 7 carrots.

_____

**9.** James bought 25 bags of chips at $3 per bag. He spent $75 in total.

_____

**10.** The delivery drivers had 236 packages to deliver. By lunchtime, they had delivered 176 packages. There were still 50 packages to deliver after lunch.

_____

| Started: | Finished: | Total Time: | Completed: | Correct: |
|---|---|---|---|---|

Name _____   Date _____

**Complete the table by squaring and cubing each number.**

|     | Number | Squared | Cubed |
|-----|--------|---------|-------|
| 1.  | 2      |         |       |
| 2.  | 3      |         |       |
| 3.  | 6      |         |       |
| 4.  | 8      |         |       |
| 5.  | 9      |         |       |

**Solve the following.**

6. $5^2 + 6^2 =$ _____

7. $8^2 - 4^2 =$ _____

8. $3^3 + 6^3 =$ _____

9. $7^2 + 2^3 - 5^2 =$ _____

10. $12^2 - 10^2 =$ _____

Name _____  Date _____

**Use >, <, or = to make each number statement true.**

**1.** 16,000,000 ☐ 1,600,000

**2.** 675,000 ☐ 6,750 × 100

**3.** 8,437,902 ☐ 8,437,956

**A car's owner's manual says to change the oil every 5,000 miles. Record the odometer readings for when the next two oil changes will be required for each of the different cars below.  The oil was changed for each of the given odometer readings.**

**4.** Car 1:  16,480 miles; _____ miles; and _____ miles

**5.** Car 2:  49,684 miles; _____ miles; and _____ miles

**6.** Car 3:  6,687 miles; _____ miles; and _____ miles

**Complete the next line in the tree diagram for each of the following.**

**7.**
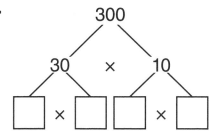

**8.**
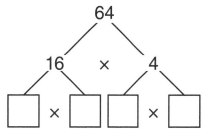

**9.**
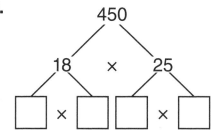

**10.**
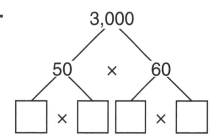

| Started: | Finished: | Total Time: | Completed: | Correct: |
|---|---|---|---|---|

Name _____   Date _____

**Write *p* to identify which of the following numbers are prime, and c to identify which are composite.**

1. 81 _____          2. 67 _____

3. 93 _____          4. 41 _____

**Circle the numbers in the chart that are evenly divisible by the given divisor.**

|     | Divisor | Possible Numbers | | | | | |
| --- | --- | --- | --- | --- | --- | --- | --- |
| 5. | 3 | 21 | 54 | 90 | 92 | 108 | 1,046 |
| 6. | 5 | 26 | 30 | 42 | 90 | 140 | 3,695 |
| 7. | 6 | 72 | 90 | 110 | 149 | 684 | 1,439 |
| 8. | 7 | 77 | 105 | 149 | 196 | 485 | 1,330 |

**Find two prime numbers that add up to the following sums.**

9. 78    _____ + _____

10. 90    _____ + _____

| Started: | Finished: | Total Time: | Completed: | Correct: |

Name _____    Date _____

**Integers are whole positive numbers or whole negative numbers. Circle the integers in each row.**

| | | | | | |
|---|---|---|---|---|---|
| **1.** | 17 | $\frac{5}{6}$ | .96 | 51% | -35 |
| **2.** | -54 | -61 | $\frac{3}{2}$ | 25 | .45 |
| **3.** | -.22 | 25% | 3.4 | -19 | 100 |
| **4.** | $3\frac{7}{10}$ | 40 | -29 | 15.2 | 98 |

**Use the number line to locate a number and to determine if the number is negative or positive.**

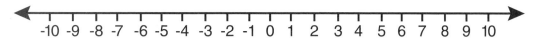

-10 -9 -8 -7 -6 -5 -4 -3 -2 -1 0 1 2 3 4 5 6 7 8 9 10

5. Two numbers to the left of 6 is _____.

6. Four numbers to the left of 10 is _____.

7. Seven numbers to the right of 2 is _____.

8. Ten numbers to the left of 5 is _____.

9. Three numbers to the left of 2 is _____.

10. Twelve numbers to the left of 6 is _____.

| Started: | Finished: | Total Time: | Completed: | Correct: |
|---|---|---|---|---|

Name _____  Date _____

**Place each set of numbers in ascending order.**

**1.** -4, -2, 8, 0, 6, -7, 9, 5 _____

**2.** -30, -16, 14, 8, 0, 2, 27, 9 _____

**Place each set of numbers in descending order.**

**3.** -4, -6, 2, 8, 0, 1, -9, 7 _____

**4.** 22, -40, 16, 0, 3, -25, 39, -14 _____

**Aidan had $45 in his bank account. What would his bank balance be if he wrote a check for:**

**5.** $16? _____

**6.** $60? _____

**7.** $43? _____

**8.** $95? _____

**Solve each equation.**

**9.** $-10 + 10 - 7 + 7 + 3 =$ _____

**10.** $5 - 2 - 6 + 4 + 1 =$ _____

| Started: | Finished: | Total Time: | Completed: | Correct: |
|----------|-----------|-------------|------------|----------|

Name _____  Date _____

## Multiply the following.

1.  30
  × 8

2.  400
  × 6

3.  8,000
  ×    5

## Complete the chart.

|     | x   | 10 | 100 | 1,000 |
| --- | --- | --- | --- | --- |
| 4. | 82 |  |  |  |
| 5. | 200 |  |  |  |
| 6. | 187 |  |  |  |

## Multiply the following.

7. 10 × 33 = _____

   20 × 33 = _____

   30 × 33 = _____

8. 10 × 60 = _____

   20 × 60 = _____

   30 × 60 = _____

9. 10 × 72 = _____

   20 × 72 = _____

   30 × 72 = _____

10. 10 × 14 = _____

    20 × 14 = _____

    30 × 14 = _____

Started:    Finished:    Total Time:    Completed:    Correct:

Name _____ Date _____

**Estimate the products of each of the following by first rounding the larger number to the nearest ten.**

1.  975
    ×   5

2.  618
    ×   7

3.  552
    ×   5

**Find the following.**

4. $16 \times 52 = (10 \times 52) + (6 \times 52) =$ _____

5. $23 \times 18 = (20 \times 18) + (3 \times 18) =$ _____

6. $43 \times 85 = (\underline{\phantom{xx}} \times 85) + (\underline{\phantom{xx}} \times 85) =$ _____

7. $32 \times 76 = (\underline{\phantom{xx}} \times 76) + (\underline{\phantom{xx}} \times 76) =$ _____

**Complete the following.**

8. $11 \times 68 =$

    68      68
    × 10    ×  1

    ____ + ____ = _____

9. $55 \times 45 =$

    45      45
    × 50    ×  5

    ____ + ____ = _____

10. $38 \times 92 =$

    92      92
    × 30    ×  8

    ____ + ____ = _____

| Started: | Finished: | Total Time: | Completed: | Correct: |
|----------|-----------|-------------|------------|----------|

Name _____ Date _____

## Circle the numbers in each row that are evenly:

**1. divisible by 2**     602          753          908          426          209          417

**2. divisible by 3**     174          765          828          1,276        6,381        9,733

**3. divisible by 5**     205          320          416          572          2,395        4,680

## True or false?

**4.** 8 is a factor of 60. _____

**5.** 4 is a factor of 32. _____

**6.** 12 is a factor of 144. _____

## Write down the first 6 factors of each number.

**7.** 24: _____, _____, _____, _____, _____, _____

**8.** 30: _____, _____, _____, _____, _____, _____

**9.** 60: _____, _____, _____, _____, _____, _____

**10.** 72: _____, _____, _____, _____, _____, _____

| Started: | Finished: | Total Time: | Completed: | Correct: |
|---|---|---|---|---|

Name _____ Date _____

**Round the first number of each problem to the nearest ten to make an estimate.**

    **1.** $52 \times 7 =$ _____

    **2.** $202 \times 6 =$ _____

**Estimate the products by rounding each number to the nearest ten before multiplying.**

    **3.** $63 \times 87 =$ _____

    **4.** $37 \times 16 =$ _____

    **5.** $61 \times 72 =$ _____

**For each problem, round the first number to the nearest ten and the second number to the nearest hundred to find an estimate.**

    **6.** $83 \times 134 =$ _____

    **7.** $24 \times 679 =$ _____

    **8.** $36 \times 865 =$ _____

**Solve the problems below.**

    **9.** Each week for 16 weeks, Jamie delivered 237 newspapers. Estimate the total number of newspapers Jamie delivered. Estimate the weeks to the nearest ten and the newspapers to the nearest hundred.

    _____

    **10.** Alyssa read 28 pages in her book every night for three weeks straight. Estimate the total number of pages Alyssa read after three weeks. Estimate the days and pages to the nearest ten.

    _____

| Started: | Finished: | Total Time: | Completed: | Correct: |
|----------|-----------|-------------|------------|----------|

Name _____ Date _____

**Find one person's equal share if these balls were shared among:**

1. 12 players _____

2. 6 coaches _____

3. 8 parents _____

**Find one share and the remainder if the soccer balls were shared among:**

4. 5 boys _____

5. 7 girls _____

6. 9 dogs _____

**Complete the division table. An example has been done for you.**

|  | Problem | Quotient | Remainder |
|---|---|---|---|
|  | 20 ÷ 3 = | 6 | 2 |
| **7.** | 30 ÷ 4 = |  |  |
| **8.** | 55 ÷ 10 = |  |  |
| **9.** | 40 ÷ 6 = |  |  |
| **10.** | 63 ÷ 5 = |  |  |

| Started: | Finished: | Total Time: | Completed: | Correct: |

Name _____ Date _____

**Divide the following. The answers do not have remainders.**

1. 4)̅1̅0̅8̅

2. 8)̅3̅6̅0̅

3. 7)̅2̅9̅4̅

4. 3)̅2̅6̅1̅

**Divide the following. The answers have remainders.**

5. 10)̅8̅6̅2̅

6. 5)̅3̅9̅7̅

7. 6)̅1̅1̅2̅

8. 8)̅3̅9̅0̅

**Solve the following word problems.**

9. Each car needs 4 tires. If there is a pile of 835 tires, how many cars can be completed?

_____

10. There were 5 dozen cupcakes at the bake sale. Nine customers bought cupcakes that day. At the end of the bake sale, there were 6 cupcakes left. If each customer bought the same number of cupcakes, how many did each one buy?

_____

| Started: | Finished: | Total Time: | Completed: | Correct: |
|---|---|---|---|---|

22

Name _____    Date _____

**How many whole pieces would each child receive if 5 children shared:**

**1.** 8 pieces of fruit? _____

**2.** 13 pieces of fruit? _____

**3.** 18 pieces of fruit? _____

**4.** 32 pieces of fruit? _____

**Divide the following and write each answer as a mixed number.**

**5.** $3\overline{)44}$

_____

**6.** $6\overline{)95}$

_____

**7.** $7\overline{)60}$

_____

**8.** $5\overline{)86}$

_____

**Divide the following and write each answer as a fraction.**

**9.** $10\overline{)7}$

_____

**10.** $3\overline{)1}$

_____

| Started: | Finished: | Total Time: | Completed: | Correct: |
| --- | --- | --- | --- | --- |

# Test 20 Multiplication and Division

Name _____ Date _____

**Divide the following. Some answers may have remainders.**

**1.** $7\overline{)7,245}$

**2.** $4\overline{)1,936}$

**3.** $10\overline{)42,681}$

**4.** $6\overline{)35,691}$

**Solve the following.**

**5.** How many students were at the game if $\frac{1}{3}$ of 6,000 students were there?

_____

**6.** If there are 7,272 gallons of water for 9 aquariums, how much water does each aquarium get?

_____

**Find the missing numbers inside the division symbols.**

**7.** $3\overline{)\underline{\phantom{236}}}$   236

**8.** $4\overline{)\underline{\phantom{602}}}$   602

**9.** $6\overline{)\underline{\phantom{720}}}$   720

**10.** $5\overline{)\underline{\phantom{391}}}$   391

| Started: | Finished: | Total Time: | Completed: | Correct: |
|---|---|---|---|---|

Name _____   Date _____

**Divide the following. The answers to these problems include remainders.**

**1.** 7)298

**2.** 12)595

**3.** 22)380

**4.** 30)999

**Solve the following word problems.**

**5.** How many cartons would 196 eggs fill if each carton holds one dozen eggs? How many eggs would be left over?

_____

**6.** If 352 toys were equally sorted into 12 boxes, how many toys would be in each box? How many toys would be left over?

_____

**Find the missing numbers inside the division symbols.**

**7.** 15) ____    18 r 1

**8.** 12) ____    47 r 10

**9.** 16) ____    25 r 3

**10.** 45) ____    16 r 9

| Started: | Finished: | Total Time: | Completed: | Correct: |
| --- | --- | --- | --- | --- |

Name _____ Date _____

**Write an improper fraction and a mixed number for the shaded part of each diagram.**

1.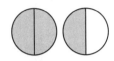

_____

2.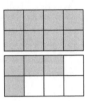

_____

3.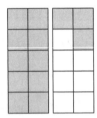

_____

4.

_____

**Write the mixed number for the following.**

5. $\frac{8}{5}$ _____

6. $\frac{9}{2}$ _____

7. $\frac{7}{3}$ _____

**Write the improper fraction for each of the following.**

8. $6\frac{1}{3}$ _____

9. $5\frac{3}{4}$ _____

10. $4\frac{4}{7}$ _____

| Started: | Finished: | Total Time: | Completed: | Correct: |
|---|---|---|---|---|

Name _____ Date _____

## Complete to make each of the following equivalent fractions.

**1.** $\dfrac{3}{4} \dfrac{(\times 2)}{(\times 2)} = \dfrac{\square}{\square}$

**2.** $\dfrac{7}{8} \dfrac{(\times 3)}{(\times 3)} = \dfrac{\square}{\square}$

**3.** $\dfrac{5}{10} \dfrac{(\div 5)}{(\div 5)} = \dfrac{\square}{\square}$

**4.** $\dfrac{18}{24} \dfrac{(\div 6)}{(\div 6)} = \dfrac{\square}{\square}$

## What number has been used to multiply the numerator and the denominator in each of the following pairs of equivalent fractions?

**5.** $\dfrac{1}{8} = \dfrac{2}{16}$ _____

**6.** $\dfrac{1}{3} = \dfrac{4}{12}$ _____

**7.** $\dfrac{3}{4} = \dfrac{12}{16}$ _____

**8.** $\dfrac{2}{3} = \dfrac{10}{15}$ _____

## Find the missing number in the equivalent fraction.

**9.** $\dfrac{3}{7} = \dfrac{\square}{28}$

**10.** $\dfrac{3}{5} = \dfrac{30}{\square}$

| Started: | Finished: | Total Time: | Completed: | Correct: |
|---|---|---|---|---|

Fractions

Name _____ Date _____

**Add the fractions. Simplify when possible.**

1. $\frac{5}{9} + \frac{3}{9} =$ _____

2. $\frac{3}{10} + \frac{2}{10} =$ _____

3. Gus and Ruby each got an apple from their mom. Gus ate $\frac{1}{4}$ of his apple. Ruby ate $\frac{3}{8}$ of her apple. What fraction of the apples did they eat altogether?

   _____

4. To follow a recipe, Molly has to add $\frac{3}{4}$ of a cup of flour and $\frac{1}{2}$ of a cup of two different kinds of sugar. How much total flour and sugar does she have to add?

   _____

**Add the fractions and then convert each answer to a mixed number. Simplify when possible.**

5. $\frac{5}{8} + \frac{5}{8} =$ _____

6. $\frac{2}{9} + \frac{8}{9} =$ _____

7. $\frac{6}{10} + \frac{9}{10} + \frac{3}{10} =$ _____

**Rewrite the fractions with common denominators before adding. Simplify and convert to mixed numbers when possible.**

8. $\frac{3}{4} + \frac{5}{12} =$ _____

9. $\frac{1}{10} + \frac{4}{5} =$ _____

10. $\frac{1}{8} + \frac{1}{2} =$ _____

| Started: | Finished: | Total Time: | Completed: | Correct: |
|---|---|---|---|---|

Name _____     Date _____

## Add the fractions. Simplify when possible.

**1.** $\frac{6}{11} + \frac{7}{11} =$ _____

**2.** $\frac{6}{14} + \frac{1}{14} =$ _____

**3.** $\frac{5}{6} + \frac{2}{3} =$ _____

**4.** $\frac{1}{4} + \frac{3}{8} =$ _____

**5.** $\frac{3}{5} + \frac{1}{10} =$ _____

## Add the mixed numbers. Simplify when possible.

**6.** $3\frac{2}{3} + 4\frac{2}{3} =$ _____

**7.** $\frac{1}{3} + 3\frac{1}{6} =$ _____

**8.** $3\frac{3}{5} + 5\frac{4}{5} =$ _____

**9.** $4\frac{3}{7} + 2\frac{4}{7} =$ _____

**10.** $5\frac{6}{7} + 6\frac{3}{14} =$ _____

| Started: | Finished: | Total Time: | Completed: | Correct: |
|---|---|---|---|---|

# Fractions

Name _____ Date _____

**Subtract the fractions. Simplify when possible.**

**1.** $\frac{9}{10} - \frac{5}{10} =$ _____

**2.** $\frac{5}{6} - \frac{4}{6} =$ _____

**3.** $\frac{7}{9} - \frac{4}{9} =$ _____

**Subtract the fractions by first rewriting them with common denominators. Simplify when possible.**

**4.** $\frac{3}{4} - \frac{2}{3} =$ _____

**5.** $\frac{7}{9} - \frac{1}{3} =$ _____

**6.** $\frac{5}{6} - \frac{3}{12} =$ _____

**Solve the following word problem.**

**7.** There were 10 slices in the birthday cake. The birthday girl ate $\frac{1}{5}$ of the cake, and 3 friends each ate one slice. How much of the cake is left?

_____

**Find the difference between the following fractions. Simplify when possible.**

**8.** $\frac{2}{3}$ and $\frac{4}{9}$ _____

**9.** $\frac{6}{10}$ and $\frac{2}{5}$ _____

**10.** $\frac{5}{8}$ and $\frac{1}{4}$ _____

| Started: | Finished: | Total Time: | Completed: | Correct: |
|---|---|---|---|---|

Name _____  Date _____

## Subtract the fractions. Simplify when possible.

1. $\dfrac{2}{4} - \dfrac{1}{8} = $ _____

2. $\dfrac{10}{11} - \dfrac{1}{2} = $ _____

3. $\dfrac{11}{12} - \dfrac{3}{9} = $ _____

4. $\dfrac{3}{5} - \dfrac{3}{12} = $ _____

5. $\dfrac{1}{2} - \dfrac{5}{11} = $ _____

## Subtract the mixed numbers. Simplify when possible.

6. $9\dfrac{5}{6} - 5\dfrac{6}{7} = $ _____

7. $4\dfrac{5}{8} - 4\dfrac{1}{12} = $ _____

8. $8\dfrac{5}{10} - 4\dfrac{2}{8} = $ _____

9. $8\dfrac{5}{6} - 1\dfrac{4}{5} = $ _____

10. $3\dfrac{1}{2} - 2\dfrac{1}{4} = $ _____

| Started: | Finished: | Total Time: | Completed: | Correct: |
|---|---|---|---|---|

Name _____  Date _____

**Write the improper fraction for the following.**

1. $3\frac{5}{10}$ _____

2. $8\frac{4}{5}$ _____

**Write the mixed number for the following.**

3. $\frac{23}{10}$ _____

4. $\frac{19}{8}$ _____

**Add the fractions.**

5. $\frac{1}{9} + \frac{2}{3} =$ _____

6. $\frac{3}{8} + \frac{1}{4} =$ _____

7. Zara has $\frac{3}{4}$ of an apple and $\frac{5}{8}$ of an orange. What is the total amount that Zara has of the two pieces of fruit?

_____

**Subtract the fractions.**

8. $\frac{9}{10} - \frac{4}{5} =$ _____

9. $\frac{11}{12} - \frac{3}{4} =$ _____

**Solve the following word problem.**

10. There are 12 slices of pizza total. Li ate 3 slices and Julia ate $\frac{1}{6}$ of the pizza. What fraction shows how many slices are left?

_____

| Started: | Finished: | Total Time: | Completed: | Correct: |

Name _____    Date _____

## Find the missing numerators.

1. $\dfrac{\phantom{0}}{5} = 6\dfrac{2}{5}$

2. $\dfrac{\phantom{0}}{8} = 2\dfrac{5}{8}$

3. $\dfrac{\phantom{0}}{10} = 7\dfrac{3}{10}$

## Use repeated addition to complete the table.

| | Problem | Repeated Addition | Fraction | Simplified Fraction |
|---|---|---|---|---|
| **4.** | $2 \times \dfrac{1}{4}$ | $\dfrac{1}{4} + \dfrac{1}{4}$ | | |
| **5.** | $4 \times \dfrac{2}{3}$ | | | |
| **6.** | $3 \times \dfrac{3}{5}$ | | | |

## Multiply the following. Simplify when possible.

7. $2 \times \dfrac{3}{10}$ _____

8. $6 \times \dfrac{3}{4}$ _____

9. The water tank holds 6,000 gallons. If $\dfrac{2}{3}$ has been removed, how many gallons were removed?

_____

10. Marco won a gift card for $300. He bought books with $\dfrac{1}{6}$ of the card. How much did he spend on books?

_____

| Started: | Finished: | Total Time: | Completed: | Correct: |
|---|---|---|---|---|

Name _____ Date _____

## Divide the fractions below. Simplify when possible.

1. $\dfrac{8}{9} \div \dfrac{3}{4} =$ _____

2. $\dfrac{1}{4} \div \dfrac{3}{8} =$ _____

3. $\dfrac{3}{8} \div 12 =$ _____

4. $\dfrac{3}{6} \div 1\dfrac{2}{3} =$ _____

5. $3\dfrac{3}{4} \div \dfrac{3}{5} =$ _____

6. $15 \div \dfrac{1}{10} =$ _____

7. $\dfrac{3}{10} \div \dfrac{12}{30} =$ _____

8. $1\dfrac{1}{2} \div 6 =$ _____

## Solve the problems below.

9. The Park Forest running club jogged 18 miles in $4\dfrac{1}{2}$ hours. How many miles did they jog per hour?

_____

10. Tiffany works in a candy shop. She made $\dfrac{5}{8}$ feet of taffy. She needs to cut it into $\dfrac{1}{4}$ foot pieces. How many pieces will she get?

_____

| Started: | Finished: | Total Time: | Completed: | Correct: |
|----------|-----------|-------------|------------|----------|

Name _____ Date _____

**Change the following fractions to mixed numbers.**

1. $\frac{7}{4}$ _____

2. $\frac{13}{8}$ _____

3. $\frac{14}{5}$ _____

**Change the following improper fractions to mixed numbers and then to decimals. Simplify the fractions when possible.**

|  | **Mixed Number** | **Decimal** |
|---|---|---|
| 4. $\frac{142}{100}$ = | _____ | = _____ |
| 5. $\frac{125}{100}$ = | _____ | = _____ |
| 6. $\frac{110}{100}$ = | _____ | = _____ |
| 7. $\frac{107}{100}$ = | _____ | = _____ |
| 8. $\frac{180}{100}$ = | _____ | = _____ |
| 9. $\frac{250}{100}$ = | _____ | = _____ |

**Solve the following word problem.**

10. Which would be more, 0.95 of a pot of gold, or $\frac{3}{5}$ of a pot of gold?

| Started: | Finished: | Total Time: | Completed: | Correct: |
|---|---|---|---|---|

Name _____  Date _____

## Add the decimals.

| 1. | 3.45 | 2. | 2.348 | 3. | 6.95 | 4. | 94.864 |
|----|------|----|-------|----|------|----|--------|
|    | + 5.84 | | + 6.395 | | 8.01 | | 4.279 |
|    |      |    |       |    | + 3.83 | | + 3.336 |

## Find the cost of the following purchases.

$98.15      $83.95      $49.50      $67.55

**5.** the shoes and the skateboard

_____

**6.** the basketball hoop and the shoes

_____

**7.** the skateboard and 2 dresses

_____

**8.** the skateboard and 2 basketball hoops

_____

## Find each total.

| 9. | $277.32 | 10. | $414.56 |
|----|---------|-----|---------|
|    | $16.54  |     | $113.19 |
|    | $19.29  |     | $47.22  |
| +  | $5.45   | +   | $3.52   |

| Started: | Finished: | Total Time: | Completed: | Correct: |
|----------|-----------|-------------|------------|----------|

*TCR 8085 Timed Math Practice*      36      ©*Teacher Created Resources*

Name _____     Date _____

## Subtract the decimals.

1. 1.16 − 0.14 =

_____

2. 5.7 − 2.4 =

_____

3.    6.95
   − 3.71
   _____

4.    2.046
   − 0.987
   _____

5.    106.2
   − 36.843
   _____

## Solve the following word problems.

6. Katie bought 5.50 feet of wire for her school project. After she was finished, there were 1.36 feet left. How much wire did Katie use?

_____

7. Mary's restaurant bill for lunch was originally $29.75. After she used a coupon, her bill was $22.30. How much did she save?

_____

## Find the difference between the following amounts.

8. $211 and $143.78 _____

9. $196.80 and $75 _____

10. $340 and $296.50 _____

| Started: | Finished: | Total Time: | Completed: | Correct: |
|---|---|---|---|---|

Name _____ Date _____

## Multiply the following.

| 1. | 6.84 | 2. | 3.63 | 3. | 16.429 | 4. | 8.765 |
|---|---|---|---|---|---|---|---|
| | × 2 | | × 8 | | × 7 | | × 4 |

## Find the cost of the following food purchases.

 $2.75       $4.26       $2.05

 $4.10       $4.39

**5.** 2 loaves of bread and a jar of jam _____

**6.** 6 packages of cookies and 2 cartons of milk _____

**7.** 1 carton of milk, 2 wedges of cheese, and a package of cookies

_____

**8.** 2 cartons of milk and 3 wedges of cheese _____

## Solve the following.

**9.** Colin's favorite cat video on the Internet has a running time of 6.25 minutes. He has watched the video 9 times. How many total minutes has he spent watching this video?

_____

**10.** Which of the following represents the best value for the money: a gallon of milk for $3.25 or a half-gallon of milk for $1.65?

_____

| Started: | Finished: | Total Time: | Completed: | Correct: |  |
|---|---|---|---|---|---|

Name _____  Date _____

## Divide the following.

**1.** 3)12.93 _____    **2.** 6)18.384 _____

**3.** 7)64.47 _____    **4.** 8)34.728 _____

## Rounding to the nearest penny, find the cost per book if each set costs:

**5.** $46.65 for 4 books. _____

**6.** $85.79 for 6 books. _____

**7.** $95.25 for 10 books. _____

## Rounding to the nearest penny, find the cost of:

**8.** 1 bar of soap if 5 cost $8.42. _____

**9.** 1 box of crackers if 3 cost $6.40. _____

**10.** 1 can of soda if 12 cost $5.11. _____

| Started: | Finished: | Total Time: | Completed: | Correct: |
|----------|-----------|-------------|------------|----------|

Name _____  Date _____

**Multiply the following decimals.**

**1.** 0.6873 × 10 = _____

**2.** 56.752 × 100 = _____

**3.** 653.105 × 1,000 = _____

**Divide the following decimals.**

**4.** 0.685 ÷ 10 = _____

**5.** 4.659 ÷ 100 = _____

**6.** 3,625.72 ÷ 1,000 = _____

**Complete the table.**

|      | × 1,000 | × 100 | × 10 | Number | ÷ 10 | ÷ 100 |
|------|---------|-------|------|--------|------|-------|
| 7.   |         |       |      | 26.43  |      |       |
| 8.   |         |       |      | 864.72 |      |       |
| 9.   |         |       |      | 25.865 |      |       |
| 10.  |         |       |      | 5.75   |      |       |

Started:     Finished:     Total Time:     Completed:     Correct:

Name _____     Date _____

## Add the decimals.

1.  6.42
    5.69
 +  7.20

2.  3.876
    5.268
 + 12.140

3.  136.75
     25.90
 +   46.17

## Find the difference between the following amounts.

**4.** $10.95 and $6.43 _____

**5.** $132.14 and $99.85 _____

## What is the total weight of the fruit?

**6.** 6 bags of oranges at 3.2 lb. each _____

**7.** 5 boxes of kiwis at 0.25 lb. each _____

**8.** 8 boxes of apples at 26.75 lb. each _____

## Divide the following.

**9.** $4\overline{)19.684}$

**10.** $8\overline{)61.320}$

| Started: | Finished: | Total Time: | Completed: | Correct: |
|----------|-----------|-------------|------------|----------|

Name _____    Date _____

**Find the decimal for the following fractions.**

**1.** $\frac{56}{100}$ _____

**2.** $\frac{1}{20}$ _____

**3.** $\frac{3}{8}$ _____

**Write the fraction for each of the following decimals.**

**4.** 0.3 _____

**5.** 0.75 _____

**6.** 0.04 _____

**Complete the table to show the fraction and decimal that represent the shaded part of each hundred square.**

| | Hundred Square | Fraction of 100 | Decimal |
|---|---|---|---|
| **7.** | | | |
| **8.** | | | |
| **9.** | | | |
| **10.** | | | |

| Started: | Finished: | Total Time: | Completed: | Correct: |
|---|---|---|---|---|

Name _____    Date _____

**Round each of the following decimals to one decimal place (tenths place).**

**1.** 5.32 _____    **2.** 25.097 _____

**Round each of the following decimals to two decimal places (hundredths place).**

**3.** 8.631 _____    **4.** 68.447 _____

**Round each of the following to the nearest whole number, and then estimate the sum.**

**5.** 13.025 + 6.785 + 102.35 _____

**6.** 3.165 + 8.927 + 65.362 _____

**7.** 22.456 + 105.987 + 62.3114 _____

**8.** 12.98 + 13.258 + 18.097 _____

**Solve the following.**

**9.** Savannah is going to pick up some groceries on her way home. She has $20 in her wallet. Does she have enough to buy all of the items listed below? Round each to the nearest dollar to estimate the total cost.

| Item | Cost | Estimate |
|------|------|----------|
| Juice | $4.48 | |
| Bread | $2.95 | |
| Milk | $3.56 | |
| Butter | $3.27 | |
| Jam | $3.79 | |

Estimate total: _____

Will Savannah have enough money to buy all her groceries? _____

**10.** Arlo and Bella bought lunch to share for $6.25, including tax. If they are splitting the cost, how much will each person pay? Round your answer to the nearest penny. _____

| Started: | Finished: | Total Time: | Completed: | Correct: |
|----------|-----------|-------------|------------|----------|

Name _____ Date _____

## How much change would be received from $40 after spending the following amounts?

**1.** $18.25 _____

**2.** $15.77 _____

**3.** $36.92 _____

**4.** $8.96 _____

## Solve the following problems.

**5.** Could Amaya buy 2 magazines for $9.95 each and 2 chocolate bars for $2.15 each with $20?

_____

**6.** What was the total cost for a pound of apples for $3.95, a bag of flour for $3.69, and 2 boxes of cereal for $4.95 each?

_____

**7.** Which is the better value—5 apples for $1.00 or a bag of 15 apples for $2.75?

_____

**8.** If Paolo bought 3 bottles of juice for $3.67 each, how much change did he receive from $20?

_____

## Find the total of each amount, then round to the nearest 5 cents.

**9.**  $6.75
$5.90
$3.25
+ $8.88

**10.**  $13.38
$4.97
$2.19
+   $4.44

| Started: | Finished: | Total Time: | Completed: | Correct: |
|---|---|---|---|---|

Name _____ Date _____

## Add the decimals.

1.    13.925
    + 3.47

2.    22.49
    + 18.305

## Find the difference between the following.

3. 4 and 2.97 _____

4. 22 and 16.815 _____

## Multiply the following.

5.   $3.75
   ×    6

6.   $7.42
   ×    4

7.   $5.36
   ×    8

## Divide the following.

8. $6.25 \div 10 =$ _____

9. $22.65 \div 100 =$ _____

10. $621.658 \div 1,000 =$ _____

| Started: | Finished: | Total Time: | Completed: | Correct: |
|---|---|---|---|---|

# Decimals

Name _____  Date _____

**Circle the larger number.**

**1.** 52 hundredths  or  one-half

**2.** 46 hundredths  or  5 tenths

**From the data bank, select a decimal to fit between the two given decimals.**

| 2.65 | 0.65 | 3.45 | 0.54 | 2.95 |
|------|------|------|------|------|

**3.** 0.5 _____ 0.6

**4.** 2.5 _____ 2.9

**Complete the following table.**

| | Decimal | $\frac{1}{10}$ larger than decimal | $\frac{1}{10}$ smaller than decimal | $\frac{1}{100}$ larger than decimal | $\frac{1}{100}$ smaller than decimal |
|-----|---------|------|------|------|------|
| **5.** | 0.5 | | | | |
| **6.** | | 0.2 | | | |
| **7.** | | | 2.45 | | |
| **8.** | | 2.16 | | | |

**Circle the largest decimal in each group.**

**9.** 5.5    1.5    15.0    12.15

**10.** 0.09    0.90    0.99    1.09

| Started: | Finished: | Total Time: | Completed: | Correct: |
|----------|-----------|-------------|------------|----------|

Name _____ Date _____

## Write the decimal equivalent to each fraction.

**1.** $\frac{40}{100}$ _____

**2.** $\frac{325}{100}$ _____

## Write the fraction in hundredths and the decimal equivalent to each common fraction.

**3.** $\frac{1}{4}$ _____

**4.** $\frac{4}{5}$ _____

**5.** $\frac{3}{20}$ _____

## Sort all the fractions from the box into their correct group of equivalents.

| | | | | |
|---|---|---|---|---|
| $\frac{2}{5}$ | 0.75 | $\frac{1}{4}$ | $\frac{3}{12}$ | $\frac{40}{100}$ |
| $\frac{1}{5}$ | $\frac{75}{100}$ | $\frac{25}{100}$ | 0.2 | $\frac{50}{100}$ |
| $\frac{4}{10}$ | 0.25 | $\frac{20}{100}$ | $\frac{3}{4}$ | $\frac{1}{2}$ |
| 0.4 | $\frac{2}{10}$ | 0.5 | $\frac{5}{10}$ | $\frac{15}{20}$ |

| | | |
|---|---|---|
| **6.** | one-fifth | |
| **7.** | two-fifths | |
| **8.** | three-fourths | |
| **9.** | one-half | |
| **10.** | one-fourth | |

| Started: | Finished: | Total Time: | Completed: | Correct: |
|---|---|---|---|---|

Name _____ Date _____

## Express the following decimals as percentages.

**1.** 0.72 _____

**2.** 0.4 _____

## Circle the greatest value in each group.

**3.**     $\frac{5}{10}$      0.62      63%

**4.**     22%      $\frac{28}{100}$      0.27

**5.**     $\frac{75}{100}$      73%      0.77

## Complete the table below.

|  | Fraction | Decimal | Percentage |
|---|---|---|---|
| **6.** | $\frac{3}{10}$ | | |
| **7.** | $\frac{6}{10}$ | | |
| **8.** | $\frac{42}{100}$ | | |
| **9.** | $\frac{34}{100}$ | | |
| **10.** | $\frac{17}{100}$ | | |

| Started: | Finished: | Total Time: | Completed: | Correct: |
|---|---|---|---|---|

Name _____    Date _____

**Express each of the following decimals as percentages.**

**1.** 0.36 _____

**2.** 0.07 _____

**Express each of the following percentages as decimals.**

**3.** 8% _____

**4.** 52% _____

**Express each of the following fractions as percentages.**

**5.** $\frac{5}{10}$ _____

**6.** $\frac{97}{100}$ _____

**Express each percentage as a fraction in its simplest form.**

**7.** 25% _____

**8.** 18% _____

**9.** 160% _____

**10.** 230% _____

| Started: | Finished: | Total Time: | Completed: | Correct: |
|----------|-----------|-------------|------------|----------|

Name _____    Date _____

## Find the number of correct answers. Round to the nearest whole number.

**1.** There were 5 questions on the history test. Taylor answered 80% of them correctly.

Taylor answered _____ questions correctly.

**2.** There were 12 questions on the science test. Samantha answered 75% of them correctly.

Samantha answered _____ questions correctly.

**3.** There were 20 questions on the social studies test. Josh answered 25% of them correctly.

Josh answered _____ questions correctly.

**4.** There were 40 questions on the language arts test. Cindy answered 50% of them correctly.

Cindy answered _____ questions correctly.

**5.** There were 10 questions on the math test. Daniel answered 90% of them correctly.

Daniel answered _____ questions correctly.

## Find the number. Round to the nearest whole number.

**6.** 35% of 25 = _____

**7.** 15% of 12 = _____

**8.** 10% of 80 = _____

**9.** 50% of 26 = _____

**10.** 70% of 15 = _____

| Started: | Finished: | Total Time: | Completed: | Correct: |
| --- | --- | --- | --- | --- |

Name _____     Date _____

## Complete the statements below. Round to the nearest tenth if necessary.

**1.** 10% of 13 is _____.

**2.** 42% of 70 is _____.

**3.** 25% of 150 is _____.

**4.** 14% of 12 is _____.

**5.** 70% of 63 is _____.

## Solve the word problems below.

**6.** On Monday, 100 sixth graders arrived at school. On Tuesday, many students had the flu and only 75% of the sixth graders arrived at school. How many students had the flu?

_____

**7.** There are 70 advertisements on the home run fence at the baseball field. A tornado damaged 30% of them and they need to be replaced. How many need to be replaced?

_____

**8.** Two hundred fifty people are expected to attend the Fourth of July picnic. Sixty percent of them will be children. How many children will attend?

_____

**9.** Of the 12 girls on the softball team, 25% are left-handed. How many girls are left-handed?

_____

**10.** Four hundred new homes are being built in town. Only 5% have swimming pools. How many have swimming pools?

_____

| Started: | Finished: | Total Time: | Completed: | Correct: |
|----------|-----------|-------------|------------|----------|

# Test 48 Order of Operations and Mixed Operations

Name _____  Date _____

**Use addition to check the subtraction equations below. If the equation is correct, make a check mark in the box to the right. If the equation is incorrect, write the correct answer in the box.**

**1.** $207 - 45 = 172$ ☐

**2.** $459 - 362 = 97$ ☐

**3.** $3,619 - 816 = 2,703$ ☐

**Use multiplication to check the division equations below. If the equation is correct, make a check mark in the box to the right. If the equation is incorrect, write the correct answer in the box.**

**4.** $580 \div 4 = 140$ ☐

**5.** $180 \div 90 = 9$ ☐

**6.** $288 \div 9 = 32$ ☐

**Check the following statements. Answer *true* or *false*.**

**7.** $187 + 49$ is less than 250 _____

**8.** $500 \times 15$ is greater than 9,000 _____

**9.** $4,095 \div 5$ is greater than 850 _____

**10.** $658 - 298$ is greater than 350 _____

| Started: | Finished: | Total Time: | Completed: | Correct: |
|---|---|---|---|---|

Name _____     Date _____

**Solve the following. Work left to right.**

**1.** $7 \times 8 \div 2 =$ _____

**2.** $75 \div 5 \times 6 =$ _____

**3.** $6 \times 8 \times 2 \div 3 =$ _____

**Solve the following. Complete the multiplication and division calculations first.**

**4.** $15 + 8 \times 9 =$ _____

**5.** $36 - 4 \times 4 =$ _____

**6.** $36 - 66 \div 3 =$ _____

**Solve the following. Complete the calculations in parentheses first, then multiply and divide, and, finally, add and subtract.**

**7.** $(7 \times 5) + 44 - 56 =$ _____

**8.** $(200 \div 5) \div (50 \div 5) =$ _____

**9.** $57 + 20 \times (14 - 8) =$ _____

**10.** $52 + (6 + 10) \div 4 =$ _____

| Started: | Finished: | Total Time: | Completed: | Correct: |
|----------|-----------|-------------|------------|----------|

Name _____  Date _____

**Solve the following. Work left to right.**

**1.** $6.8 \div 4 \times 2 =$ _____

**2.** $3.6 \div 6 \times 5 =$ _____

**3.** $0.7 \times 9 \div 3 =$ _____

**Solve the following. Multiply and divide before adding and subtracting.**

**4.** $5.6 \times 4 + 8 \times 1.2 =$ _____

**5.** $50 + 30 \div 3 - 8.1 =$ _____

**6.** $100 \div 20 - 5 \times 0.3 =$ _____

**Solve the following. Complete the calculations in parentheses first, then multiply and divide, and, finally, add and subtract.**

**7.** $(\frac{1}{2} + \frac{3}{4}) \times 16 =$ _____

**8.** $\frac{1}{6} \times (40 - 4) =$ _____

**9.** $(\frac{1}{3} \times 14) \times 6 =$ _____

**10.** $4 - (\frac{2}{10} + \frac{3}{10}) + 1\frac{1}{2} =$ _____

| Started: | Finished: | Total Time: | Completed: | Correct: |
|---|---|---|---|---|

Name _____    Date _____

**Solve the following.**

1. $(804 + 101) - (476 + 187) =$ _____

2. $\frac{7}{4} + \frac{5}{4} + 15 =$ _____

3. $0.68 + 4.8 + 0.19 - 1.6 =$ _____

4. $(200 \div 4) \times 16 =$ _____

5. $72 \div 9 + (7 \times 8) =$ _____

6. $(25 \times 4) \div (45 \div 9) =$ _____

**Write each of the following as an equation and solve it.**

7. *W* is 16 more than the product of 8, 6, and 9.

_____

8. *X* is the sum of 15, 16, and 17, divided by 6.

_____

9. *Y* is the answer to 15 multiplied by 7, divided by 3, and then added to 12.

_____

10. If I add 14 and 36 together, then divide by 10 and add 4, I get *Z*.

_____

Name _____ Date _____

**Round each of the following amounts to the nearest 5 cents.**

1. $6.82 _____

2. $3.99 _____

**Add or subtract the following amounts.**

3.     $4.65
      $3.82
  + $13.79

4.     $95.98
   − $16.61

**Multiply or divide the following.**

5.    $8.65
  ×    3

6. $5)\overline{\$12.75}$

**Find the change from $20.00 if I spent:**

7. $14.83 _____

8. $5.62 _____

9. $8.11 _____

10. $9.29 _____

| Started: | Finished: | Total Time: | Completed: | Correct: |
|---|---|---|---|---|

Name _____  Date _____

**Write *true* or *false* for each of the given answers.**

1. $(16 \times \blacksquare) + 12 = 40$

   $\blacksquare = 2$ _____

2. $12 + (4 \times \bigstar) = 56$

   $\bigstar = 5$ _____

3. $41 - (7 \times \blacklozenge) = 6$

   $\blacklozenge = 5$ _____

**Find the missing number in each of the following.**

4. _____ $- 37 = 23$       5. $5 \times$ _____ $= 75$

6. (_____ $\div 3) + 25 = 49$       7. $(4 \times$ _____$) - 42 = 22$

**Find the number (N) if I:**

8. subtract 12 from it, then divide by 6. The answer is 12.

   _____

9. divide it in half, then add 36. The answer is 50.

   _____

10. add 100, then divide by 5. The answer is 40.

   _____

| Started: | Finished: | Total Time: | Completed: | Correct: |
|---|---|---|---|---|

Name _____ Date _____

## Find the missing numbers.

**1.** 56 + 135 = 126 + _____

**2.** 198 + 235 = 360 + _____

**3.** 1,210 ÷ _____ = 10 × 11

**4.** 12 × _____ = 432 ÷ 3

**5.** 100 ÷ _____ = 25 – 5

**6.** 144 ÷ 6 = 6 × _____

## What was the starting number (N) if I:

**7.** multiplied by 8, added 429, then divided by 5 to get 105?

_____

**8.** added 57, multiplied by 2, then divided by 20 to get 11?

_____

**9.** subtracted 6, multiplied by 5, then added 9 to get 34?

_____

**10.** divided by 3, added 17, then multiplied by 3 to get 90?

_____

| Started: | Finished: | Total Time: | Completed: | Correct: |
|----------|-----------|-------------|------------|----------|

Name _____   Date _____

## Remember the order of operations:

```
1 Parentheses
2 Exponents
3 Multiply/Divide
  from left to right
4 Add/Subtract
  from left to right
```

## Solve each problem.

**1.** $10 + (8 \times 2) =$ _____

**2.** $(10 \div 5) - 2 =$ _____

**3.** $(9 \div 3) + 9 - 10 =$ _____

**4.** $5 + (6 \times 7) - 3 =$ _____

**5.** $(5 \times 4) + 3 - 4 =$ _____

**6.** $(4^2 + 5) \div 3 =$ _____

**7.** $(8 + 9) - (9 - 2^2) =$ _____

**8.** $(24 \div 8) \times 3 - 7 =$ _____

**9.** $8 \times (16 \div 8) + 2 =$ _____

**10.** $(42 + 33) - 40 =$ _____

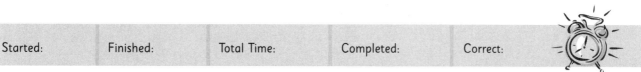

| Started: | Finished: | Total Time: | Completed: | Correct: |
| --- | --- | --- | --- | --- |

Name _____ Date _____

## Find the sum.

**1.**  -3
    -4
+ -2
_____

**2.**  -2.3
    -5
+  10
_____

**3.**  -8
    7
   -9
+  4
_____

## Find the difference.

**4.** $3.6 - 8 = $ _____

**5.** $2 - 9 = $ _____

**6.** $-30 - (-80) = $ _____

## Find the difference or sum.

**7.** $5 - (-5) - (-6) = $ _____

**8.** $9 - 7 - (-5) = $ _____

**9.** $(2 - 8) - 8 - (9 - 4) = $ _____

**10.** $(7 - 3) - (7 - 11) + 7 = $ _____

| Started: | Finished: | Total Time: | Completed: | Correct: |
|---|---|---|---|---|

Name _____   Date _____

## Multiply the following.

**1.** -11 × -6.2 = _____

**2.** -1 × -20 × 5 = _____

**3.** (7 − 3) × -3 × -2 = _____

## Divide the following.

**4.** 21 ÷ -7 = _____

**5.** -72 ÷ -8 = _____

**6.** (3 − 12) ÷ (9 − 6) = _____

## Find the answers to the following.

**7.** $\dfrac{-81 \times (-3 + 6)}{9}$ = _____

**8.** $\dfrac{90 \times (2 - 5)}{-5}$ = _____

**9.** $\dfrac{2 \times (1 - 6) - 7 \times (2 + 3)}{-9 \times (3 - 4)}$ = _____

**10.** $\dfrac{8 \times (-10 + 7) + 4 \times (27 - 36)}{4 \times (5 - 2)}$ = _____

| Started: | Finished: | Total Time: | Completed: | Correct: |
|---|---|---|---|---|

Name _____    Date _____

## Name each object. Use the shape names in the box to help you.

| triangular prism | rectangular prism | triangular pyramid | cube | pentagonal prism |
|---|---|---|---|---|

**1.** _____

**2.** _____

**3.** _____

**4.** _____

**5.** _____

## Complete the table below.

| | Object | Faces | Edges | Vertices |
|---|---|---|---|---|
| **6.** | cube | | | |
| **7.** | rectangular prism | | | |
| **8.** | triangular prism | | | |
| **9.** | square pyramid | | | |
| **10.** | triangular pyramid | | | |

| Started: | Finished: | Total Time: | Completed: | Correct: |
|---|---|---|---|---|

Name _____  Date _____

## List the shapes (number and type) that make up a:

**1.** square pyramid. _____

**2.** hexagonal prism. _____

**3.** cube. _____

**4.** rectangular pyramid. _____

**5.** triangular prism. _____

**6.** rectangular prism. _____

## Name the 3D objects that are constructed from the following shapes.

**7.** 1 hexagon and 6 triangles _____

**8.** 4 triangles _____

**9.** 2 octagons and 8 rectangles _____

**10.** 2 squares and 4 rectangles _____

| Started: | Finished: | Total Time: | Completed: | Correct: |
| --- | --- | --- | --- | --- |

Name _____ Date _____

a.　　　　b.　　　　c.　　　　d.

## Which of the shapes above could be viewed from a different angle as:

**1.** _____

**2.** _____

**3.**  _____

**4.**  _____

**5.** _____

**6.** _____

## Write the name of the container used in each stack.

**7.** 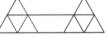 _____

**8.**  _____

**9.**  _____

**10.**  _____

| Started: | Finished: | Total Time: | Completed: | Correct: |
|---|---|---|---|---|

Name _____      Date _____

## Name each of the following objects.

**1.**  _____

**2.**  _____

**3.**  _____

**4.**  _____

**5.**  _____

**6.**  _____

## Complete the table.

|  | Shape | Side View of Shape | Number of Edges | Number of Surfaces | Number of Vertices | Number of Curved Surfaces | Does it Roll? |
|---|---|---|---|---|---|---|---|
| **7.** | Cube | | | | | | |
| **8.** | Sphere | | | | | | |
| **9.** | Cone | | | | | | |
| **10.** | Cylinder | | | | | | |

| Started: | Finished: | Total Time: | Completed: | Correct: |
|---|---|---|---|---|

Name _____  Date _____

## Name the 3D object that each net makes.

1.  _____

2.  _____

3.  _____

4. 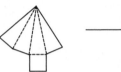 _____

5.  _____

6.  _____

## Draw the top view of the following shapes:

| **7.** triangular pyramid | **8.** rectangular prism |
|---|---|
| **9.** cone | **10.** cube |

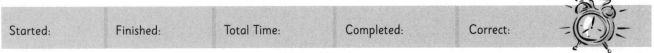

| Started: | Finished: | Total Time: | Completed: | Correct: |
|---|---|---|---|---|

Name _____     Date _____

## What is the direction halfway between:

**1.** north and south? _____

**2.** north and west? _____

**3.** south and east? _____

## If you are facing north, what direction is:

**4.** behind you? _____

**5.** to your right? _____

**6.** to your left? _____

## Using the grid, name the shape that is:

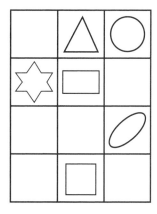

**7.** south of the rectangle. _____     **8.** northwest of the oval. _____

**9.** west of the circle. _____     **10.** northeast of the star. _____

| Started: | Finished: | Total Time: | Completed: | Correct: |
|---|---|---|---|---|

Name _____ Date _____

**Give the coordinates for the positions of the children marked on the map.**

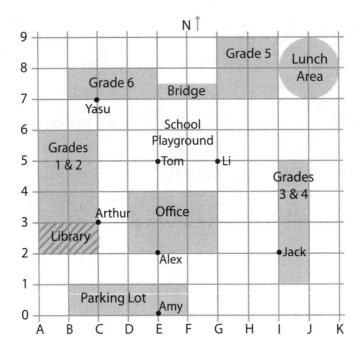

**1.** Amy _____

**2.** Arthur _____

**3.** Li _____

**4.** Jack _____

**5.** Tom _____

**6.** Yasu _____

**Mark the following coordinates on the map.**

**7.** (D, 6)

**8.** (G, 7)

**9.** (F, 3)

**10.** (A, 6)

| Started: | Finished: | Total Time: | Completed: | Correct: |
|----------|-----------|-------------|------------|----------|

Name _____      Date _____

## Name the state that is located at the following coordinates on the grid.

**1.** (I, 9) _____

**2.** (C, 6) _____

**3.** (P, 6) _____

## Give the main direction to:

**4.** New Mexico from Colorado. _____

**5.** Tennessee from Alabama. _____

**6.** Colorado from Utah. _____

## Write the name of the state you would be in if you started at:

**7.** (J, 1) and traveled north 4 lines. _____

**8.** (G, 5) and traveled east 5 lines. _____

**9.** (F, 9) and traveled south 2 lines. _____

**10.** (J, 5) and traveled west 5 lines. _____

| Started: | Finished: | Total Time: | Completed: | Correct: |
| --- | --- | --- | --- | --- |

Name _____ Date _____

## Complete the table.

| | Diagram | Length (in.) | Width (in.) | Area (in.²) |
|---|---|---|---|---|
| **1.** | 7, 3 | | | |
| **2.** | 5, 5 | | | |
| **3.** | 6, 2 | | | |
| **4.** | 12, 5 | | | |

## Calculate the area of each of the following shapes.

**5.**   9 cm, 12 cm      _____

**6.**  9 in.      _____

**7.** 1.5 ft., 1 ft.      _____

**8.**  11 ft., 9 ft.      _____

**9.**  5 in., 8 in.      _____

**10.** 4 cm, 8 cm      _____

| Started: | Finished: | Total Time: | Completed: | Correct: |
|---|---|---|---|---|

Name _____  Date _____

**Complete the following table by finding the area of each rectangle and then dividing by 2 to find the area of one of its triangles.**

| | Diagram | Area of Rectangle (in.²) | Area of Triangle (in.²) |
|---|---|---|---|
| **1.** | 8 in. / 3 in. | | |
| **2.** | 10 in. / 9 in. | | |
| **3.** | 8 in. / 8 in. | | |
| **4.** | 5 in. / 4 in. | | |
| **5.** | 6 in. / 2 in. | | |

**Find the area of each triangle.**

**6.**

7 ft. / 7 ft.

_____

**7.**

9 in. / 2 in.

_____

**8.**

8 cm / 6 cm

_____

**9.**
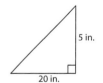
5 in. / 20 in.

_____

**10.**

4 cm / 5 cm

_____

| Started: | Finished: | Total Time: | Completed: | Correct: |  |
|---|---|---|---|---|---|

Name _____    Date _____

**Select the most suitable unit (in.³ or ft.³) to find the volume of the following.**

**1.** a mobile phone _____

**2.** a classroom _____

**3.** an ice cream container _____

**What is the volume of each of the following in cubic units (units³)?**

**4.**

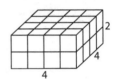

_____

**5.**

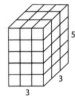

_____

**6.**

_____

**7.**

_____

**Find the volume of each of the following prisms (measurements in inches).**

**8.**

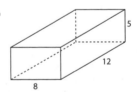

_____

**9.**

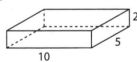

_____

**10.**

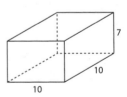

_____

| Started: | Finished: | Total Time: | Completed: | Correct: |
|---|---|---|---|---|

Name _____ Date _____

## Find the volume for each solid.

**1.**

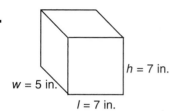

$h$ = 7 in.
$w$ = 5 in.
$l$ = 7 in.

_____ × _____ × _____

= _____

**2.**

$s$ = 1 ft.

_____³ = _____

**3.**

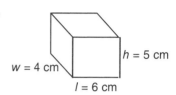

$h$ = 5 cm
$w$ = 4 cm
$l$ = 6 cm

_____ × _____ × _____

= _____

**4.**

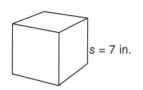

$s$ = 7 in.

_____³ = _____

**5.**

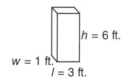

$h$ = 6 ft.
$w$ = 1 ft.
$l$ = 3 ft.

_____ × _____ × _____

= _____

**6.**

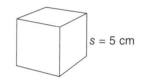

$s$ = 5 cm

_____³ = _____

## Complete the table.

|      | Length (cm) | Width (cm) | Height (cm) | Volume (cm³) |
|------|-------------|------------|-------------|--------------|
| **7.**  | 4 | 2 | 6 |  |
| **8.**  | 7 | 3 | 5 |  |
| **9.**  | 3 | 2 | 2 |  |
| **10.** | 4 | 2 | 1 |  |

| Started: | Finished: | Total Time: | Completed: | Correct: |

Name _____  Date _____

## Complete the table.

| | Diagram | Length (cm) | Width (cm) | Height (cm) | Volume (cm³) |
|---|---|---|---|---|---|
| **1.** | 6 cm, 3 cm, 4 cm | | | | |
| **2.** | 3 cm, 2 cm, 2 cm | | | | |
| **3.** | 2 cm, 1 cm, 4 cm | | | | |
| **4.** | 2 cm, 4 cm, 5 cm | | | | |

## Calculate the volume of each of the following prisms.

**5.**
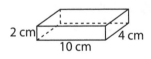
2 cm · 10 cm · 4 cm

_____

**6.**

2 cm · 6 cm · 7 cm

_____

**7.**

7 cm · 4 cm · 3 cm

_____

**8.**

4 cm · 4 cm · 5 cm

_____

**9.**
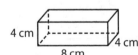
4 cm · 8 cm · 4 cm

_____

**10.**
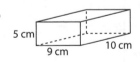
5 cm · 9 cm · 10 cm

_____

| Started: | Finished: | Total Time: | Completed: | Correct: |
|---|---|---|---|---|

Name _____     Date _____

## Draw each of the following times on the clock faces.

**1.** quarter to 4

**2.** half past 6

**3.** 11 o'clock

## Write each of the following times in words.

**4.**

_____

**5.**

_____

**6.**

_____

## Solve the following.

**7.** Lunchtime begins at 5 minutes past 12. If there are $2\frac{3}{4}$ hours left of school, what time will the bell ring to go home?

_____

## Find the difference between a quarter past 2 a.m. and the time shown. All times are in a.m.

**8.**

_____

**9.**

_____

**10.**

_____

| Started: | Finished: | Total Time: | Completed: | Correct: |
|----------|-----------|-------------|------------|----------|

Name _____     Date _____

## Write each of the following in digital time.

**1.**

_____

**2.**

_____

## For each of the following digital times, write *morning*, *afternoon*, or *evening*.

**3.**

_____

**4.**

_____

**5.**

_____

## Find the difference between:

**6.** 3:15 p.m. and 8:50 p.m. _____

**7.** 10:16 a.m. and 2:05 p.m. _____

**8.** 11:05 a.m. and 7:47 p.m. _____

## Order the times from earliest in the day to latest.

**9.** 2:31 p.m., 2:33 a.m., 2:32 p.m. _____

**10.** 9:16 a.m., 4:37 p.m., 11:22 a.m. _____

| Started: | Finished: | Total Time: | Completed: | Correct: |
| --- | --- | --- | --- | --- |

Name _____     Date _____

## If it is noon at Greenwich, what is the time at the following longitudes?

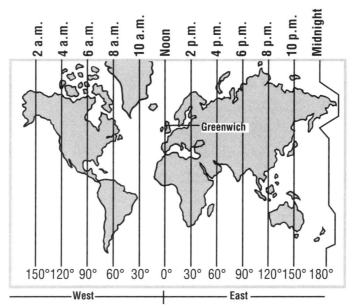

**1.** 60° west _____

**2.** 90° east _____

**3.** 150° east _____

## If it is 8:00 p.m. at Greenwich, what is the time at the following longitudes?

**4.** 30° west _____

**5.** 120° east _____

**6.** 150° west _____

## It is midnight in Australia (150°E). Give the time in:

**7.** Greenland (30° W) _____

**8.** China (105° E) _____

## Find the time at Greenwich if it is noon in:

**9.** Cuba (75° W) _____

**10.** Indonesia (120° E) _____

| Started: | Finished: | Total Time: | Completed: | Correct: |
|---|---|---|---|---|

Name _____   Date _____

## What do each of these stopwatch times mean?

**1.** 06:16.19 _____

**2.** 12:32.09 _____

**3.** 00:07.54 _____

## Circle the faster (shorter) time in each pair.

|     | Time 1 | Time 2 |
|-----|--------|--------|
| **4.** | 00:09.27 | 00:09.54 |
| **5.** | 04:16.65 | 04:26.33 |

## Circle the slower (longer) time in each pair.

|     |          |          |
|-----|----------|----------|
| **6.** | 35:16.42 | 35:28.83 |
| **7.** | 04:17.19 | 04:08.52 |

## Write the difference in time between the following.

**8.** 28:12.43 and 28:14.28 _____

**9.** 02:59.46 and 03:00.56 _____

**10.** 41:37.56 and 42:45.58 _____

| Started: | Finished: | Total Time: | Completed: | Correct: |
|----------|-----------|-------------|------------|----------|

Name _____    Date _____

**Mark the beginning of each of the tropical cyclones on the timeline.**

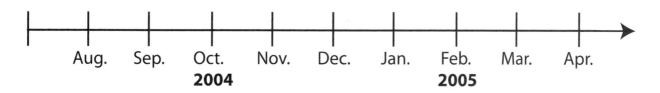

Aug.   Sep.   Oct.   Nov.   Dec.   Jan.   Feb.   Mar.   Apr.

**2004**                     **2005**

**1.** Phoebe: August 31        **2.** Raymond: December 31

**3.** Sally: January 7        **4.** Tim: January 23

**5.** Vivienne: February 5        **6.** Ingrid: March 5

**How many days were between the beginnings of the following tropical cyclones?**

**7.** Raymond and Sally _____

**8.** Sally and Tim _____

**9.** Raymond and Tim _____

**10.** Sally and Vivienne _____

| Started: | Finished: | Total Time: | Completed: | Correct: |
| --- | --- | --- | --- | --- |

Name _____ Date _____

## Give each of the following as an average speed (mph).

**1.** 50 miles in 30 minutes _____

**2.** 270 miles in 3 hours _____

**3.** 180 miles in 4 hours _____

## Give the distance traveled in:

**4.** 5 hours at 75 mph _____

**5.** $2\frac{1}{2}$ hours at 70 mph _____

**6.** 45 minutes at 88 mph _____

## Complete the following table.

|  | Distance | Time | Average Speed |
|---|---|---|---|
| **7.** | 30 miles | 1 hour | |
| **8.** | 100 miles | | 50 mph |
| **9.** | 1 mile | 10 minutes | |
| **10.** | | 3 hours | 80 mph |

| Started: | Finished: | Total Time: | Completed: | Correct: |
|---|---|---|---|---|

Name _____ Date _____

## Find the average (mean) of each group of numbers.

**1.** 16, 42, 98, 101 _____

**2.** $10, $14, $15, $18, $24 _____

**3.** 150, 170, 190, 200, 210 _____

**Below are the temperatures at noon for one week. What is the average (mean) temperature at noon for:**

| Day | Mon. | Tues. | Wed. | Thurs. | Fri. | Sat. | Sun. |
|---|---|---|---|---|---|---|---|
| Temp °F | 86 | 88 | 84 | 89 | 80 | 77 | 79 |

**4.** Monday and Tuesday? _____

**5.** Wednesday, Saturday, and Sunday? _____

**6.** the weekdays? _____

**7.** the weekend? _____

## What is the average (mean) number of:

**8.** marbles in jars of 116, 126, and 130? _____

**9.** pieces of fruit in baskets of 12, 18, 22, and 24? _____

**10.** toothpicks in boxes of 300, 325, 350, and 400? _____

| Started: | Finished: | Total Time: | Completed: | Correct: |
|---|---|---|---|---|

Name _____  Date _____

**Which of the spinners has the greatest chance of landing on the following colors?**

| **A.** | **B.** | **C.** | **D.** | **E.** | **F.** |
|---|---|---|---|---|---|
|  |  |  |  |  |  |

**1.** white (W) _____

**2.** red (R) _____

**3.** green (G) _____

**4.** orange (O) _____

**5.** yellow (Y) _____

**6.** blue (B) _____

**Write the probability of each spinner landing on blue (B) as a fraction.**

**7.**   _____

**8.**   _____

**9.**   _____

**10.**   _____

| Started: | Finished: | Total Time: | Completed: | Correct: |
|---|---|---|---|---|

Name _____  Date _____

**Use the scale 0 to 1 to rate the chance of the following events happening.**

1. My first toss of a coin will be tails. _____

2. I will fly to the moon next week. _____

3. The sun will rise tomorrow. _____

4. My classmate's birthday is in a month that starts with J.

    _____

**There are 10 colored balls in the box. State the probability of drawing each color combination as a decimal.**

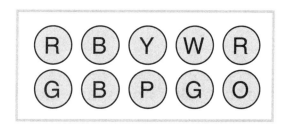

5. yellow (Y) _____

6. red (R) _____

7. red (R) or blue (B) _____

8. blue (B) or orange (O) _____

9. pink (P) or white (W) _____

10. white (W), yellow (Y), or green (G) _____

| Started: | Finished: | Total Time: | Completed: | Correct: |
| --- | --- | --- | --- | --- |

Name _____  Date _____

## Fifty children were surveyed to find their favorite color.

| red | blue | yellow | green | orange | pink | black |
|-----|------|--------|-------|--------|------|-------|
| 10  | 10   | 6      | 8     | 5      | 3    | 8     |

**Use the information above to predict how many children out of 200 would prefer the following colors:**

1. blue _____

2. black _____

3. pink _____

4. yellow _____

5. orange _____

6. red _____

7. green _____

**Use the information above to predict how many children out of 500 would prefer the following colors:**

8. blue _____

9. green _____

10. pink _____

| Started: | Finished: | Total Time: | Completed: | Correct: |
|----------|-----------|-------------|------------|----------|

Name _____  Date _____

**Mrs. Carney surveyed all of the students in her class to find out their main use for the computer. Their use was email (E), Internet (I), games (G), and homework (H). Here is the data for the class:**

| E, I, G, E, H, H, I, G, G, G, E, E, E, G, I, H, E, G, G, I, H, E, E, G, G, H |
|---|

**Complete a tally table based on the above information.**

|   | Computer Use | Tally |
|---|---|---|
| **1.** | email |  |
| **2.** | Internet |  |
| **3.** | games |  |
| **4.** | homework |  |

**Using the information from the tally table, determine how many students mainly used the computer for:**

5. email? _____

6. homework? _____

7. games? _____

8. Internet? _____

9. email or Internet? _____

10. games or homework? _____

Name _____ Date _____

On the table, there were 30 blocks lined up in a row. Erica drew the divided bar graph below 15 cm long so that each $\frac{1}{2}$ cm stood for one block.

| blue | green | yellow | red |
|------|-------|--------|-----|

Measure in centimeters to determine the length that each color represents on the graph.

**1.** yellow blocks _____

**2.** red blocks _____

**3.** green blocks _____

**4.** blue blocks _____

**5.** red or yellow blocks _____

**6.** blue or green blocks _____

**What fraction of the graph shows the following?**

**7.** red blocks _____

**8.** yellow blocks _____

**9.** blue blocks _____

**10.** green blocks _____

| Started: | Finished: | Total Time: | Completed: | Correct: |
|----------|-----------|-------------|------------|----------|

Name _____  Date _____

For a school of 200 students, this is the breakdown of students in winter sports. Complete the table using the information from the pie chart.

| | Sport | Fraction | Percent | Number |
|---|---|---|---|---|
| **1.** | football | | 37.5% | 75 |
| **2.** | gymnastics | $\frac{1}{8}$ | 12.5% | |
| **3.** | indoor soccer | | | 50 |
| **4.** | basketball | $\frac{1}{4}$ | | |

For the same school of 200 students, this is the breakdown of students in summer sports. Complete the table using the information from the pie chart.

| | Sport | Fraction | Percent | Number |
|---|---|---|---|---|
| **5.** | baseball | | | |
| **6.** | basketball | | | |
| **7.** | tennis | | | |
| **8.** | soccer | | | |
| **9.** | swimming | | | |
| **10.** | softball | | | |

Started: _____  Finished: _____  Total Time: _____  Completed: _____  Correct: _____

Name _____    Date _____

## Find the mean of each set of measurements.

**1.** 33 in., 17 in., 42 in., 26 in.

**2.** 75°, 70°, 73°, 80°

_____    _____

**3.** 66 cm, 50 cm, 55 cm, 36 cm, 18 cm

**4.** 96 ft., 87 ft., 72 ft., 67 ft., 88 ft.

_____    _____

**5.** 650 lb., 880 lb., 475 lb., 495 lb.

_____

## Find the median of the following values.

**6.** 2, 4, 6, 8, 10

**7.** 1, 3, 5, 7, 9, 11, 13

_____    _____

**8.** 40, 60, 80, 100, 120

**9.** 320, 450, 490, 510

_____    _____

**10.** 1.2, 1.8, 2.3, 3.5, 4.6, 5.2

_____

| Started: | Finished: | Total Time: | Completed: | Correct: |

Name _____    Date _____

**Water, oil, and detergent were used to fill a 1,000 mL container. In the container, what is the volume of:**

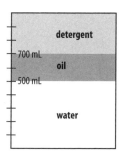

1. detergent? _____

2. water? _____

3. oil? _____

**What fraction of the container has:**

4. water? _____

5. oil? _____

6. detergent? _____

**This divided bar graph shows the breakdown of the most popular types of pets. Exactly 500 people were surveyed. How many people preferred:**

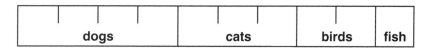

7. dogs? _____

8. birds? _____

9. fish? _____

10. cats? _____

| Started: | Finished: | Total Time: | Completed: | Correct: |
|----------|-----------|-------------|------------|----------|

Name _____ Date _____

**Isabel travels 630 miles by car every year to visit her cousins. Find the time it takes her to travel:**

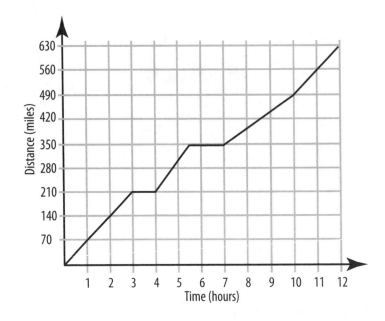

**1.** 490 miles. _____

**2.** 280 miles. _____

**3.** 70 miles. _____

**4.** 630 miles. _____

**5.** 350 miles. _____

**How far does Isabel travel in:**

**6.** 7 hours? _____

**7.** 10 hours? _____

**8.** 3 hours? _____

**9.** 4 hours? _____

**10.** 1 hour? _____

| Started: | Finished: | Total Time: | Completed: | Correct: |
|---|---|---|---|---|

Name _____ Date _____

**The following graph shows how we can convert between Celsius and Fahrenheit temperatures. Use the graph to convert:**

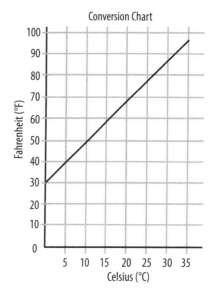

**1.** 10°C to °F. _____

**2.** 90°F to °C. _____

**3.** 35°C to °F. _____

**Circle the greater temperature.**

**4.**       25°C       or       80°F

**5.**       20°C       or       60°F

**6.**       5°C       or       35°F

**Jordan drew a pie graph to show what he does during his school day.**

**7.** What activity took up the least time?

_____

**8.** What activities took up the most time?

_____

**9.** Was more time spent writing or doing science?

_____

**10.** Was less time spent in reading or art?

_____

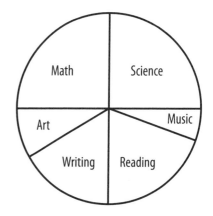

| Started: | Finished: | Total Time: | Completed: | Correct: |
|---|---|---|---|---|

Name _____   Date _____

## Use the population graph to answer the following.

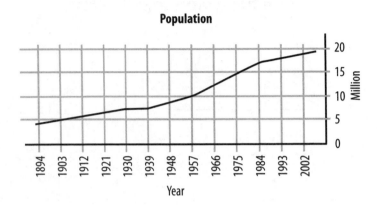

**Population**

**When was the population approximately:**

**1.** 5 million? _____

**2.** 7 million? _____

**3.** 12 million? _____

**4.** 15 million? _____

**5.** 18 million? _____

## What was the approximate population:

**6.** in 1980? _____

**7.** in 1930? _____

**8.** in 1990? _____

**9.** difference between 1900 and 2000? _____

**10.** difference between 1900 and 1950? _____

| Started: | Finished: | Total Time: | Completed: | Correct: |
|----------|-----------|-------------|------------|----------|

Name _____  Date _____

**Find the answer to each of the following problems.**

1. Bill can walk 3 miles in 45 minutes. How long would it take Bill to walk 10 miles? _____

2. Marcella can jog a mile every 6 minutes. How many miles can Marcella jog in 30 minutes? _____

3. Andrew can rollerblade 1 block every 15 seconds. How many blocks can Andrew rollerblade in 2 minutes? _____

4. Yuko drove 40 miles per hour. How long will it take Yuko to drive 100 miles? _____

5. The jet flies 750 miles per hour. How many minutes will it take the jet to fly 150 miles? _____

6. It takes Olivia 30 seconds to count to 25. How many minutes will it take her to count to 300? _____

7. Jason packs eggs at a rate of 2 cartons every 3 minutes. How many cartons can he pack in 45 minutes? _____

8. Bella can read 5 words every 12 seconds. How many words can she read in 1 minute? _____

9. Louisa can scoop 3 scoops of ice cream every 8 seconds. How many whole scoops can Louisa scoop in 1 minute? _____

10. Rico can do 140 jumping jacks in 2 minutes. How many jumping jacks can Rico do in 7 minutes? _____

| Started: | Finished: | Total Time: | Completed: | Correct: |
|---|---|---|---|---|

Name _____   Date _____

A school fundraiser sold exactly 600 raffle tickets. The winner will receive a new laptop. Jared bought 13 raffle tickets. Lewis bought 10 raffle tickets. What is the fraction that shows the probability that:

**1.** Jared will win the laptop? _____

**2.** Lewis will win the laptop? _____

**3.** Jared or Lewis will win the laptop? _____

Julie bought 17 of the raffle tickets. What is the fraction that shows the probability that:

**4.** Julie will win the laptop? _____

I have a die with the numbers 1 through 6 on it. What is the fraction that shows the probability:

**5.** of rolling a 4 or 5? _____

**6.** of rolling a 1, 5, or 6? _____

**7.** of rolling a 2, 3, 4, or 6? _____

I have a die with the numbers 1 through 12 on it. What is the fraction that shows the probability:

**8.** of rolling a 4 or 7? _____

**9.** of rolling a 3, 8, or 11? _____

**10.** of rolling a 1, 2, 3, 4, or 7? _____

| Started: | Finished: | Total Time: | Completed: | Correct: |
| --- | --- | --- | --- | --- |

Name _____      Date _____

**Solve for _x_ and then check your answer in the problems below. An example has been done for you.**

$x - 5 = 14$
$x - 5 + 5 = 14 + 5$
$x = 19$

**Check:**
$19 - 5 = 14$
$14 = 14$

**1.** $x - 7 = 25$

**2.** $7 + x = 19$

**3.** $x - 4 = 20$

**4.** $8 + x = 15$

**5.** $9 + x = 9$

**6.** $x + 6 = 21$

**7.** $x - 12 = 17$

**8.** $15 + x = 31$

**9.** $x - 22 = 4$

**10.** $16 + x = 40$

| Started: | Finished: | Total Time: | Completed: | Correct: | |
|---|---|---|---|---|---|

Name _____    Date _____

**Rewrite each problem and solve it.**

$$n = 10$$

**1.** $2 \times n =$ _____

**2.** $n \div 2 =$ _____

**3.** $8 + n =$ _____

**4.** $n - 9 =$ _____

**Add the missing sign (+, −, ×, ÷) to make each equation true. Rewrite the equation and solve it.**

$$s = 9$$

**5.** $4 \boxed{\phantom{x}} s = 36$ _____

**6.** $s \boxed{\phantom{x}} 10 = 19$ _____

**7.** $s \boxed{\phantom{x}} 8 = 72$ _____

**8.** $s \boxed{\phantom{x}} 7 = 2$ _____

**9.** $5 \boxed{\phantom{x}} s = 14$ _____

**10.** $s \boxed{\phantom{x}} 3 = 3$ _____

| Started: | Finished: | Total Time: | Completed: | Correct: |
|---|---|---|---|---|

Name _____    Date _____

## Find the value of each letter.

**1.** $B + B + B + B = 240$ _____

**2.** $Y + 19 = 31$ _____

**3.** $\frac{1}{3}$ of $A = 18$ _____

## Write an equation for each of the following and solve it.

**4.** Multiply 6 by 30 and subtract five times seven.

_____

**5.** Add 15 to nine, multiply by three, and then divide by eight.

_____

**6.** Square 4 and add to the product of 8 and 7.

_____

## Complete the table.

| | ★ | ◆ | ★ + ◆ | ★ − ◆ |
|---|---|---|---|---|
| **7.** | 6.3 | 4.2 | | |
| **8.** | 8.2 | | 9.9 | |
| **9.** | | 5.3 | | 4.5 |
| **10.** | 10.8 | | 16.8 | |

| Started: | Finished: | Total Time: | Completed: | Correct: |

Name _____   Date _____

**Solve for each variable in the following equations.**

**1.** $V - 7 = 83$ _____

**2.** $8 \times 8 = M^2$ _____

**3.** $K - 8.6 = 9$ _____

**4.** $11 \times F = 90 - 24$ _____

**Solve each of the following equations.**

**5.** $T = (49 \div 7) + 20$ _____

**6.** $E = 36 \div (3 \times 2)$ _____

**7.** $(3 \times 15) - (2 \times 5) = Z$ _____

**Write an equation for each of the following and solve it. Use G for each unknown number.**

**8.** Five friends went to the movies. If the total cost of the tickets was $66.50, how much did each ticket cost?

_____

**9.** Kelly had some apples, 4 oranges, and 6 lemons. If she had 13 pieces of fruit, how many apples did she have?

_____

**10.** The chocolates are divided into 4 rows of 3 for each tray. If there are 60 chocolates, how many trays are needed?

_____

| Started: | Finished: | Total Time: | Completed: | Correct: |
|---|---|---|---|---|

Name _____ Date _____

**Write the algebraic expression. If there is one variable, use *x*. If there are two variables, use *x* and *y*.**

    **1.** 10 less than a number _____

    **2.** 4 times a number plus 5 times another number _____

    **3.** the sum of 6 and a number divided by 10 _____

**Change the algebraic expressions to statements in words.**

    **4.** $4y$ _____

    **5.** $2y - 5$ _____

**Combine the like terms to simplify each expression.**

    **6.** $3y + y =$ _____

    **7.** $2 + 3n - 7 =$ _____

    **8.** $5r - 2r =$ _____

    **9.** $4x - 3x + 1 =$ _____

  **10.** $\frac{8}{2}x - 9y - 6x + 12y =$ _____

| Started: | Finished: | Total Time: | Completed: | Correct: |
|---|---|---|---|---|

Name _____ Date _____

## Evaluate the following expressions.

**Let $n = 6$, $s = 5$, and $t = 2$**

   **1.** $3n + 6s =$ _____

   **2.** $9n - 4t =$ _____

   **3.** $2n - 3s + 10 =$ _____

**Let $a = -3$, $b = 4$, and $c = 2$**

   **4.** $ac - b =$ _____

   **5.** $4b - 2c - 3a =$ _____

   **6.** $7(c + b) =$ _____

## Answer the question below.

   **7.** The temperature outside is 59°F. What is it in Celsius? Use this formula:

      $C = \dfrac{5}{9} \times (F - 32)$ _____

## Solve each equation using an inverse operation.

   **8.** $y + 20 = 100$ _____

   **9.** $24 = a - 18$ _____

  **10.** $-25 = \dfrac{a}{5}$ _____

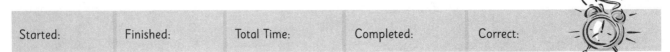

| Started: | Finished: | Total Time: | Completed: | Correct: |
| --- | --- | --- | --- | --- |

Name _____     Date _____

## Solve these two- and three-step equations.

**1.** $8a - 4 = 60$ _____

**2.** $9z - 12 = 69$ _____

**3.** $39 = 14d - 3$ _____

## Combine the variables to solve the equations.

**4.** $3x - 2x - 10 = -9$

_____

**5.** $14x - 10 - 4x = 0$

_____

**6.** $x + 2x + 3x = 12$

_____

**7.** $8x + 2 + 2x = 32$

_____

## Solve these equations with variables on each side.

**8.** $4x = 8 + 2x$

_____

**9.** $3a + 10 = 8a$

_____

**10.** $5r + 32 = 8r + 17$

_____

| Started: | Finished: | Total Time: | Completed: | Correct: |
|----------|-----------|-------------|------------|----------|

Name _____     Date _____

**Solve the following equations by simplifying to remove the parentheses.**

**1.** $5(x + 2) = 25$ _____

**2.** $5(x + 3) = 6(x - 4)$ _____

**3.** $7(b + 2) = 28$ _____

**4.** $4(x - 2) = 72$ _____

**5.** $2(4x + 11) = -3 + 3x$ _____

**6.** $3(2 + x) = -10 + 2x$ _____

**Solve the following equations for the indicated variable.**

**7.** $c + d + y = b$     Solve for $y$.     _____

**8.** $x - c = r$     Solve for $x$.     _____

**9.** $a + b = n$     Solve for $a$.     _____

**10.** $dx = b$     Solve for $x$.     _____

| Started: | Finished: | Total Time: | Completed: | Correct: |
|---|---|---|---|---|

Name _____    Date _____

## Find the coordinates for the points on the graph.

**1.** Point A = ( _____, _____ )

**2.** Point B = ( _____, _____ )

**3.** Point C = ( _____, _____ )

**4.** Point D = ( _____, _____ )

**5.** Point E = ( _____, _____ )

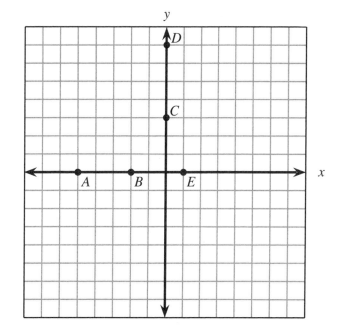

## Find the coordinates for the points on the graph.

**6.** Point F = ( _____, _____ )

**7.** Point G = ( _____, _____ )

**8.** Point H = ( _____, _____ )

**9.** Point I = ( _____, _____ )

**10.** Point J = ( _____, _____ )

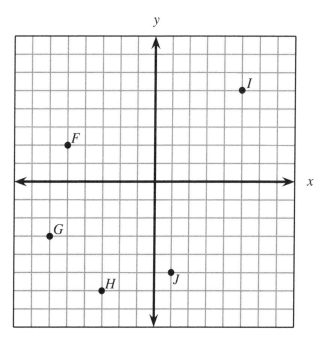

| Started: | Finished: | Total Time: | Completed: | Correct: |
|---|---|---|---|---|

Name _____    Date _____

## Graph the possible solutions for the equations.

$$y = 2x - 8$$

|      | x  | y |
|------|----|---|
| 1.   | 2  |   |
| 2.   | 4  |   |
| 3.   | 6  |   |
| 4.   | 8  |   |

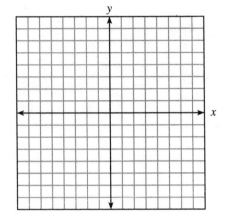

$$y = x - 3$$

|      | x  | y |
|------|----|---|
| 5.   | -2 |   |
| 6.   | 5  |   |
| 7.   | 6  |   |

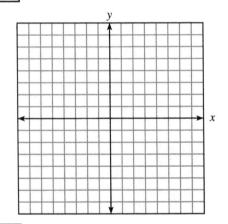

$$y = \frac{1}{2}x + 1$$

|      | x  | y |
|------|----|---|
| 8.   | -6 |   |
| 9.   | 2  |   |
| 10.  | 6  |   |

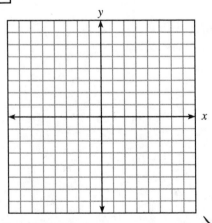

| Started: | Finished: | Total Time: | Completed: | Correct: |
|----------|-----------|-------------|------------|----------|

# Standards

Pages in *Timed Math Practice* meet one or more of the following Common Core State Standards.

© Copyright 2010. National Governors Association Center for Best Practices and Council of Chief State School Officers. All rights reserved. For more information about the Common Core State Standards, go to **http://www.corestandards.org**

| Mathematics Standards | Test |
|---|---|
| **Ratios and Proportional Relationships** | |
| Understand ratio concepts and use ratio reasoning to solve problems. | 38, 44, 45, 46, 76, 89 |
| **The Number System** | |
| Apply and extend previous understandings of multiplication and division to divide fractions by fractions. | 23, 30 |
| Compute fluently with multi-digit numbers and find common factors and multiples. | 2, 3, 4, 5, 6, 7, 8, 9, 10, 13, 14, 15, 16, 17, 18, 19, 20, 21, 22, 24, 25, 26, 27, 28, 29, 31, 32, 33, 34, 35, 36, 37, 39, 40, 41, 42, 43, 47, 48, 49, 50, 52, 55, 71, 72, 73, 74 |
| Apply and extend previous understandings of numbers to the system of rational numbers. | 11, 12, 56, 57 |
| **Expressions and Equations** | |
| Apply and extend previous understandings of arithmetic to algebraic expressions. | 1, 7, 8, 53, 54, 95, 96, 97, 98 |
| Reason about and solve one-variable equations and inequalities. | 51, 91, 92, 93, 94 |
| **Geometry** | |
| Solve real-world and mathematical problems involving area, surface area, and volume. | 59, 60, 61, 62, 64, 65, 66, 67, 68, 69, 70 |
| **Statistics and Probability** | |
| Summarize and describe distributions. | 75, 77, 78, 79, 80, 81, 82, 83, 84, 85, 86, 87, 88, 90, 99, 100 |

# Answer Key

## Test 1—Page 5
1. 42; 48; Rule: multiply by 6
2. 55; 65; 75; Rule: multiply by 10
3. 7; 9; 10; Rule: divide by 9
4. 1; 1 1/2; 2; Rule: divide by 2
5. 19; 24; 30
6. 66; 59; 53
7. 7; 9.5; 12.5
8. 28; 39; 52
9. 9; 13; 17; 21; 25
10. 9; 12; 15; 18; 21

## Test 2—Page 6
1. 1,043,275
2. 1,608,739
3. 806,540
4. $1,016,641
5. $980,742
6. $954,300
7. 27,468 feet
8. 20,244 pounds
9. 1,253,508.4
10. one million, two hundred fifty-three thousand, five hundred eight and four tenths

## Test 3—Page 7
1. 900
2. 400
3. 1,000
4. 3,000
5. 6,000 + 2,000; 8,000
6. 5,000 + 6,000; 11,000
7. 36,000 + 10,000; 46,000
8. false
9. false
10. true

## Test 4—Page 8
1. 78,168
2. 23,169
3. 17,668
4. 56,000 − 36,000 = 20,000
5. 88,000 − 22,000 = 66,000
6. 302,928 inches
7. 346,194 feet
8. 446,427 yards
9. 235,195 miles
10. $178,332

## Test 5—Page 9
1. 3,073,920
2. 6,046,849
3. 394,687 mi.$^2$
4. 87,449 mi.$^2$
5. 108,071 mi.$^2$
6. 97,940 mi.$^2$
7. 158,020 mi.$^2$
8. 652,336 mi.$^2$
9. $1,760,727
10. $10,653,553

## Test 6—Page 10
1. 25,700 + 29,200 = 54,900
2. 42,400 + 10,400 = 52,800
3. 278,300 + 308,900 = 587,200
4. 104,600 + 307,900 = 412,500
5. 47,000 − 19,000 = 28,000
6. 32,000 − 10,000 = 22,000
7. 256,000 − 125,000 = 131,000
8. 801,000 − 623,000 = 178,000
9. $626 + $42 = $668
10. $884 − $367 = $517

## Test 7—Page 11
1. false
2. true
3. true
4. false
5. 4
6. 1
7. 4
8. false; Each horse should receive 8 carrots.
9. true
10. false; There were 60 packages left to deliver.

## Test 8—Page 12
1. 4; 8
2. 9; 27
3. 36; 216
4. 64; 512
5. 81; 729
6. 61
7. 48
8. 243
9. 32
10. 44

## Test 9—Page 13
1. >
2. =
3. <
4. 21,480 and 26,480
5. 54,684 and 59,684
6. 11,687 and 16,687
7. answers will vary, possible answers: 5 × 6 and 5 × 2
8. answers will vary, possible answers: 4 × 4 and 2 × 2
9. answers will vary, possible answers: 6 × 3 and 5 × 5
10. answers will vary, possible answers: 10 × 5 and 10 × 6

## Test 10—Page 14
1. c
2. p
3. c
4. p
5. 21; 54; 90; 108
6. 30; 90; 140; 3,695
7. 72; 90; 684
8. 77; 105; 196; 1,330
9. answers will vary, possible answers: 73 + 5, 71 + 7, 67 + 11, 61 + 17, 59 + 19, 47 + 31, 41 + 37
10. answers will vary, possible answers: 83 + 7, 79 + 11, 73 + 17, 71 + 19, 67 + 23, 61 + 29, 59 + 31, 53 + 37, 47 + 43

## Test 11—Page 15
1. 17, -35
2. -54, -61, 25
3. -19, 100
4. 40, -29, 98
5. 4
6. 6
7. 9
8. -5
9. -1
10. -6

## Test 12—Page 16
1. -7, -4, -2, 0, 5, 6, 8, 9
2. -30, -16, 0, 2, 8, 9, 14, 27
3. 8, 7, 2, 1, 0, -4, -6, -9
4. 39, 22, 16, 3, 0, -14, -25, -40
5. $29
6. -$15
7. $2
8. -$50
9. 3
10. 2

## Test 13—Page 17
1. 240
2. 2,400
3. 40,000
4. 820; 8,200; 82,000
5. 2,000; 20,000; 200,000
6. 1,870; 18,700; 187,000
7. 330; 660; 990
8. 600; 1,200; 1,800
9. 720; 1,440; 2,160
10. 140; 280; 420

## Test 14—Page 18
1. 4,900
2. 4,340

3. 2,750
4. 832
5. 414
6. 40; 3; 3,655
7. 30; 2; 2,432
8. 680 + 68 = 748
9. 2,250 + 225 = 2,475
10. 2,760; 736; 3,496

**Test 15—Page 19**
1. 602; 908; 426
2. 174; 765; 828; 6,381
3. 205; 320; 2,395; 4,680
4. false
5. true
6. true
7. 1, 2, 3, 4, 6, 8
8. 1, 2, 3, 5, 6, 10
9. 1, 2, 3, 4, 5, 6
10. 1, 2, 3, 4, 6, 8

**Test 16—Page 20**
1. 50 × 7 = 350
2. 200 × 6 = 1,200
3. 60 × 90 = 5,400
4. 40 × 20 = 800
5. 60 × 70 = 4,200
6. 80 × 100 = 8,000
7. 20 × 700 = 14,000
8. 40 × 900 = 36,000
9. 20 × 200 = 4,000 newspapers
10. 30 × 20 = 600 pages

**Test 17—Page 21**
1. 2
2. 4
3. 3
4. 4 r 4
5. 3 r 3
6. 2 r 6
7. 7, 2
8. 5, 5
9. 6, 4
10. 12, 3

**Test 18—Page 22**
1. 27
2. 45
3. 42
4. 87
5. 86 r 2
6. 79 r 2
7. 18 r 4
8. 48 r 6
9. 208 cars
10. 6 cupcakes

**Test 19—Page 23**
1. 1
2. 2
3. 3
4. 6
5. 14 2/3
6. 15 5/6
7. 8 4/7
8. 17 1/5
9. 7/10
10. 1/3

**Test 20—Page 24**
1. 1,035
2. 484
3. 4,268 r 1
4. 5,948 r 3
5. 2,000 students
6. 808 gallons
7. 708
8. 2,408
9. 4,320
10. 1,955

**Test 21—Page 25**
1. 42 r 4
2. 49 r 7
3. 17 r 6
4. 33 r 9
5. 16 cartons, 4 eggs left over
6. 29 toys, 4 toys left over
7. 271
8. 574
9. 403
10. 729

**Test 22—Page 26**
1. 3/2, 1 1/2
2. 12/8 or 3/2, 1 4/8 or 1 1/2
3. 13/10, 1 3/10
4. 9/4 or 2 1/4
5. 1 3/5
6. 4 1/2
7. 2 1/3
8. 19/3
9. 23/4
10. 32/7

**Test 23—Page 27**
1. 6/8
2. 21/24
3. 1/2
4. 3/4
5. 2
6. 4
7. 4
8. 5
9. 12

10. 50

**Test 24—Page 28**
1. 8/9
2. 5/10 or 1/2
3. 5/8
4. 1 3/4 cups
5. 10/8 = 1 1/4
6. 10/9 = 1 1/9
7. 18/10 = 1 4/5
8. 9/12 + 5/12 = 14/12 = 1 1/6
9. 1/10 + 8/10 = 9/10
10. 1/8 + 4/8 = 5/8

**Test 25—Page 29**
1. 1 2/11
2. 1/2
3. 1 1/2
4. 5/8
5. 7/10
6. 8 1/3
7. 3 1/2
8. 9 2/5
9. 7
10. 12 1/14

**Test 26—Page 30**
1. 2/5
2. 1/6
3. 1/3
4. 9/12 – 8/12 = 1/12
5. 7/9 – 3/9 = 4/9
6. 10/12 – 3/12 = 7/12
7. 1/2 or 5 slices
8. 2/9
9. 1/5
10. 3/8

**Test 27—Page 31**
1. 3/8
2. 9/22
3. 7/12
4. 7/20
5. 1/22
6. 3 41/42
7. 13/24
8. 4 1/4
9. 7 1/30
10. 1 1/4

**Test 28—Page 32**
1. 35/10
2. 44/5
3. 2 3/10
4. 2 3/8
5. 7/9
6. 5/8
7. 1 3/8
8. 1/10
9. 1/6
10. 7/12

**Test 29—Page 33**
1. 32

**2.** 21

**3.** 73

**4.** 2/4; 1/2

**5.** 2/3 + 2/3 + 2/3 + 2/3; 8/3; 2 2/3

**6.** 3/5 + 3/5 + 3/5; 9/5; 1 4/5

**7.** 3/5

**8.** 9/2 or 4 1/2

**9.** 4,000 gallons

**10.** $50

## Test 30—Page 34

**1.** 1 5/27

**2.** 2/3

**3.** 1/32

**4.** 3/10

**5.** 6 1/4

**6.** 150

**7.** 3/4

**8.** 1/4

**9.** 4 miles per hour

**10.** 2 1/2 pieces

## Test 31—Page 35

**1.** 1 3/4

**2.** 1 5/8

**3.** 2 4/5

**4.** 1 21/50, 1.42

**5.** 1 1/4, 1.25

**6.** 1 1/10, 1.10

**7.** 1 7/100, 1.07

**8.** 1 4/5, 1.80

**9.** 2 1/2, 2.50

**10.** 0.95 of a pot of gold would be more

## Test 32—Page 36

**1.** 9.29

**2.** 8.743

**3.** 18.79

**4.** 102.479

**5.** $165.70

**6.** $151.50

**7.** $197.15

**8.** $266.05

**9.** $318.60

**10.** $578.49

## Test 33—Page 37

**1.** 1.02

**2.** 3.3

**3.** 3.24

**4.** 1.059

**5.** 69.357

**6.** 4.14 feet

**7.** $7.45

**8.** $67.22

**9.** $121.80

**10.** $43.50

## Test 34—Page 38

**1.** 13.68

**2.** 29.04

**3.** 115.003

**4.** 35.06

**5.** $9.76

**6.** $28.70

**7.** $14.93

**8.** $17.27

**9.** 56.25 minutes

**10.** a gallon of milk for $3.25

## Test 35—Page 39

**1.** 4.31

**2.** 3.064

**3.** 9.21

**4.** 4.341

**5.** $11.66

**6.** $14.30

**7.** $9.53

**8.** $1.68

**9.** $2.13

**10.** $0.43

## Test 36—Page 40

**1.** 6.873

**2.** 5,675.2

**3.** 653,105

**4.** 0.0685

**5.** 0.04659

**6.** 3.62572

**7.** 26,430; 2,643; 264.3; 2.643; 0.2643

**8.** 864,720; 86,472; 8,647.2; 86.472; 8.6472

**9.** 25,865; 2,586.5; 258.65; 2.5865; 0.25865

**10.** 5,750; 575; 57.5; 0.575; 0.0575

## Test 37—Page 41

**1.** 19.31

**2.** 21.284

**3.** 208.82

**4.** $4.52

**5.** $32.29

**6.** 19.2 lb.

**7.** 1.25 lb.

**8.** 214 lb.

**9.** 4.921

**10.** 7.665

## Test 38—Page 42

**1.** 0.56

**2.** 0.05

**3.** 0.375

**4.** 3/10

**5.** 75/100 or 3/4

**6.** 4/100 or 1/25

**7.** 25/100 or 1/4, 0.25

**8.** 80/100 or 4/5, 0.80

**9.** 52/100 or 13/25, 0.52

**10.** 73/100, 0.73

## Test 39—Page 43

**1.** 5.3

**2.** 25.1

**3.** 8.63

**4.** 68.45

**5.** 13 + 7 + 102 = 122

**6.** 3 + 9 + 65 = 77

**7.** 22 + 106 + 62 = 190

**8.** 13 + 13 + 18 = 44

**9.** $4.00, $3.00, $4.00, $3.00, $4.00

Estimate total: $18.00

yes

**10.** $3.13

## Test 40—Page 44

**1.** $21.75

**2.** $24.23

**3.** $3.08

**4.** $31.04

**5.** no

**6.** $17.54

**7.** 15 apples for $2.75

**8.** $8.99

**9.** $24.78, $24.80

**10.** $24.98, $25.00

## Test 41—Page 45

**1.** 17.395

**2.** 40.795

**3.** 1.03

**4.** 5.185

**5.** $22.50

**6.** $29.68

**7.** $42.88

**8.** 0.625

**9.** 0.2265

**10.** 0.621658

## Test 42—Page 46

**1.** 52 hundredths

**2.** 5 tenths

**3.** 0.54

**4.** 2.65

**5.** 0.6, 0.4, 0.51, 0.49

**6.** 0.1, 0, 0.11, 0.09

**7.** 2.55, 2.65, 2.56, 2.54

**8.** 2.06, 1.96, 2.07, 2.05

**9.** 15.0

**10.** 1.09

## Test 43—Page 47

**1.** 0.40

**2.** 3.25

**3.** 25/100, 0.25

4. 80/100, 0.80
5. 15/100, 0.15
6. 1/5, 20/100, 2/10, 0.2
7. 2/5, 40/100, 4/10, 0.4
8. 3/4, 75/100, 15/20, 0.75
9. 1/2, 50/100, 5/10, 0.5
10. 1/4, 25/100, 3/12, 0.25

**Test 44—Page 48**
1. 72%
2. 40%
3. 63%
4. 28/100
5. 0.77
6. 0.3, 30%
7. 0.6, 60%
8. 0.42, 42%
9. 0.34, 34%
10. 0.17, 17%

**Test 45—Page 49**
1. 36%
2. 7%
3. 0.08
4. 0.52
5. 50%
6. 97%
7. 1/4
8. 9/50
9. 1 3/5
10. 2 3/10

**Test 46—Page 50**
1. 4
2. 9
3. 5
4. 20
5. 9
6. 8 3/4, 9
7. 1 4/5, 2
8. 8
9. 13
10. 10 1/2, 11

**Test 47—Page 51**
1. 1.3
2. 29.4
3. 37.5
4. 1.7
5. 44.1
6. 25 students
7. 21 advertisements
8. 150 children
9. 3 girls
10. 20 homes have pools

**Test 48—Page 52**
1. 162

2. ✓
3. 2,803
4. 145
5. 2
6. ✓
7. true
8. false
9. false
10. true

**Test 49—Page 53**
1. 28
2. 90
3. 32
4. 87
5. 20
6. 14
7. 23
8. 4
9. 177
10. 56

**Test 50—Page 54**
1. 3.4
2. 3
3. 2.1
4. 32
5. 51.9
6. 3.5
7. 20
8. 6
9. 28
10. 5

**Test 51—Page 55**
1. 242
2. 18
3. 4.07
4. 800
5. 64
6. 20
7. W = 16 + (8 × 6 × 9), W = 448
8. X = (15 + 16 + 17) ÷ 6, X = 8
9. Y = 15 × 7 ÷ 3 + 12, Y = 47
10. (14 + 36) ÷ 10 + 4 = Z, Z = 9

**Test 52—Page 56**
1. $6.80
2. $4.00
3. $22.26
4. $79.37
5. $25.95
6. $2.55
7. $5.17
8. $14.38
9. $11.89
10. $10.71

**Test 53—Page 57**
1. false
2. false
3. true
4. 60
5. 15
6. 72
7. 16
8. N = 84
9. N = 28
10. N = 100

**Test 54—Page 58**
1. 65
2. 73
3. 11
4. 12
5. 5
6. 4
7. N = 12
8. N = 53
9. N = 11
10. N = 39

**Test 55—Page 59**
1. 26
2. 0
3. 2
4. 44
5. 19
6. 7
7. 12
8. 2
9. 18
10. 35

**Test 56—Page 60**
1. -9
2. 2.7
3. -6
4. -4.4
5. -7
6. 50
7. 16
8. 7
9. -19
10. 15

**Test 57—Page 61**
1. 68.2
2. 100
3. 24
4. -3
5. 9
6. -3
7. -27
8. 54
9. -5

**10.** -5

**Test 58—Page 62**
1. triangular prism
2. pentagonal prism
3. cube
4. rectangular prism
5. triangular pyramid
6. 6, 12, 8
7. 6, 12, 8
8. 5, 9, 6
9. 5, 8, 5
10. 4, 6, 4

**Test 59—Page 63**
1. 1 square, 4 triangles
2. 2 hexagons, 6 rectangles
3. 6 squares
4. 1 rectangle, 4 triangles
5. 2 triangles, 3 rectangles
6. 6 rectangles
7. hexagonal pyramid
8. triangular pyramid
9. octagonal prism
10. square prism

**Test 60—Page 64**
1. c
2. a
3. b and d
4. d
5. b and c
6. b
7. triangular prism
8. cube
9. cylinder
10. rectangular prism

**Test 61—Page 65**
1. cone
2. sphere
3. cone
4. cylinder
5. cylinder
6. cylinder
7. square, 12, 6, 8, 0, no
8. circle, 0, 1, 0, 1, yes
9. triangle or circle, 1, 2, 1, 1, yes
10. rectangle or circle, 2, 3, 0, 1, yes

**Test 62—Page 66**
1. pentagonal prism
2. hexagonal prism
3. triangular pyramid
4. square pyramid
5. triangular prism

6. rectangular prism
7. △ or △ 8. ☐
9. ⊙ 10. ☐

**Test 63—Page 67**
1. east or west
2. northwest
3. southeast
4. south
5. east
6. west
7. square
8. rectangle, triangle, or star
9. triangle
10. triangle or circle

**Test 64—Page 68**
1. (E, 0)
2. (C, 3)
3. (G, 5)
4. (I, 2)
5. (E, 5)
6. (C, 7)
7.–10. Check map.

**Test 65—Page 69**
1. North Dakota
2. Nevada
3. Ohio
4. south
5. north
6. east
7. Kansas
8. Missouri
9. Wyoming
10. Utah

**Test 66—Page 70**
1. 7 in., 3 in., 21 in$^2$
2. 5 in., 5 in., 25 in$^2$
3. 6 in., 2 in., 12 in$^2$
4. 12 in., 5 in., 60 in$^2$
5. 108 cm$^2$
6. 81 in.$^2$
7. 1.5 ft.$^2$
8. 99 ft.$^2$
9. 40 in.$^2$
10. 32 cm$^2$

**Test 67—Page 71**
1. 24 in$^2$, 12 in$^2$
2. 90 in$^2$, 45 in$^2$
3. 64 in$^2$, 32 in$^2$
4. 20 in$^2$, 10 in$^2$
5. 12 in$^2$, 6 in$^2$
6. 24.5 ft.$^2$
7. 9 in.$^2$
8. 24 cm$^2$

9. 50 in.$^2$
10. 10 cm$^2$

**Test 68—Page 72**
1. in.$^3$
2. ft.$^3$
3. in.$^3$
4. 32 units$^3$
5. 45 units$^3$
6. 6 units$^3$
7. 12 units$^3$
8. 480 in$^3$
9. 100 in$^3$
10. 700 in$^3$

**Test 69—Page 73**
1. 7 in. x 5 in. x 7 in. = 245 in.$^3$
2. (1 ft.)$^3$ = 1 ft.$^3$
3. 6 cm x 4 cm x 5 cm = 120 cm$^3$
4. (7 in.)$^3$ = 343 in.$^3$
5. 3 ft. x 6 ft. x 1 ft. = 18 ft.$^3$
6. (5 cm)$^3$ = 125 cm$^3$
7. 48 cm$^3$
8. 105 cm$^3$
9. 12 cm$^3$
10. 8 cm$^3$

**Test 70—Page 74**
1. 4 cm, 3 cm, 6 cm, 72 cm$^3$
2. 2 cm, 2 cm, 3 cm, 12 cm$^3$
3. 4 cm, 2 cm, 1 cm, 8 cm$^3$
4. 5 cm, 2 cm, 4 cm, 40 cm$^3$
5. 80 cm$^3$
6. 84 cm$^3$
7. 84 cm$^3$
8. 80 cm$^3$
9. 128 cm$^3$
10. 450 cm$^3$

**Test 71—Page 75**
1. check drawing
2. check drawing
3. check drawing
4. two twenty or twenty minutes past two
5. seven fifty or ten minutes to eight
6. ten thirty-five or twenty-five minutes to eleven
7. 2:50
8. 2 hours, 15 minutes
9. 5 hours, 10 minutes
10. 3 hours, 30 minutes

**Test 72—Page 76**
1. 1:34
2. 2:17

3. evening
4. morning
5. afternoon
6. 5 hours, 35 minutes
7. 3 hours, 49 minutes
8. 8 hours, 42 minutes
9. 2:33 a.m., 2:31 p.m., 2:32 p.m.
10. 9:16 a.m., 11:22 a.m., 4:37 p.m.

## Test 73—Page 77
1. 8:00 a.m.
2. 6:00 p.m.
3. 10:00 p.m.
4. 6:00 p.m.
5. 4:00 a.m.
6. 10:00 a.m.
7. 12:00 noon
8. 9:00 p.m.
9. 5:00 p.m.
10. 4:00 a.m.

## Test 74—Page 78
1. 6 minutes, 16.19 seconds
2. 12 minutes, 32.09 seconds
3. 7.54 seconds
4. 00:09.27
5. 04:16.65
6. 35:28.83
7. 04:17.19
8. 1.85 seconds
9. 1.10 seconds
10. 1 minute, 8.02 seconds

## Test 75—Page 79
1.–6.

7. 7 days
8. 16 days
9. 23 days
10. 29 days

## Test 76—Page 80
1. 100 mph
2. 90 mph
3. 45 mph
4. 375 miles
5. 175 miles
6. 66 miles
7. 30 mph
8. 2 hours
9. 6 mph
10. 240 miles

## Test 77—Page 81
1. 64.25

2. $16.20
3. 184
4. 87°F
5. 80°F
6. 85.4°F
7. 78°F
8. 124 marbles
9. 19 pieces of fruit
10. 343.75 toothpicks

## Test 78—Page 82
1. A
2. D
3. B
4. C
5. E
6. F
7. 2/8 or 1/4
8. 4/8 or 1/2
9. 3/8
10. 1/8

## Test 79—Page 83
1. 0.5
2. 0
3. 1
4. 0.2–0.3
5. 0.1
6. 0.2
7. 0.4
8. 0.3
9. 0.2
10. 0.4

## Test 80—Page 84
1. 40
2. 32
3. 12
4. 24
5. 20
6. 40
7. 32
8. 100
9. 80
10. 30

## Test 81—Page 85
1. ⅂ℍ Ⅲ
2. ⅠⅠⅠⅠ
3. ⅂ℍ ⅠⅠⅠⅠ
4. ⅂ℍ
5. 8
6. 5
7. 9
8. 4
9. 12
10. 14

## Test 82—Page 86
1. 2 cm
2. 6 cm
3. 2 cm
4. 5 cm
5. 8 cm
6. 7 cm
7. 6/15 or 2/5
8. 2/15
9. 5/15 or 1/3
10. 2/15

## Test 83—Page 87
1. 3/8
2. 25
3. 1/4, 25%
4. 25%, 50
5. 1/4, 25%, 50
6. 1/4, 25%, 50
7. 1/8, 12.5%, 25
8. 1/8, 12.5%, 25
9. 1/8, 12.5%, 25
10. 1/8, 12.5%, 25

## Test 84—Page 88
1. 29.5 in.
2. 74.5°
3. 45 cm
4. 82 ft.
5. 625 lb.
6. 6
7. 7
8. 80
9. 470
10. 2.9

## Test 85—Page 89
1. 300 mL
2. 500 mL
3. 200 mL
4. 1/2
5. 2/10 or 1/5
6. 3/10
7. 200
8. 100
9. 50
10. 150

## Test 86—Page 90
1. 10 hours
2. about 4 3/4 hours
3. 1 hour
4. 12 hours
5. 5 1/2 hours
6. 350 miles
7. 490 miles
8. 210 miles
9. 210 miles

**10.** 70 miles

**Test 87—Page 91**
1. 50°F
2. about 32°C
3. about 95°F
4. 80°F
5. 20°C
6. 5°C
7. music
8. math and science
9. science
10. art

**Test 88—Page 92**
1. 1903
2. around 1921
3. around 1966
4. between 1975 and 1984
5. around 2002
6. about 16 million
7. about 7 million
8. about 17 million
9. about 14 million
10. about 4 million

**Test 89—Page 93**
1. 150 minutes
2. 5 miles
3. 8 blocks
4. 2.5 hours
5. 12 minutes
6. 6 minutes
7. 30 cartons
8. 25 words
9. 22 scoops
10. 490 jumping jacks

**Test 90—Page 94**
1. 13/600
2. 10/600
3. 23/600
4. 17/600
5. 2/6 or 1/3
6. 3/6 or 1/2
7. 4/6 or 2/3
8. 2/12 or 1/6
9. 3/12 or 1/4
10. 5/12

**Test 91—Page 95**
1. $x = 32, 32 - 7 = 25, 25 = 25$
2. $x = 12, 7 + 12 = 19, 19 = 19$
3. $x = 24, 24 - 4 = 20, 20 = 20$
4. $x = 7, 8 + 7 = 15, 15 = 15$
5. $x = 0, 9 + 0 = 9, 9 = 9$
6. $x = 15, 15 + 6 = 21, 21 = 21$
7. $x = 29, 29 - 12 = 17, 17 = 17$

8. $x = 16, 15 + 16 = 31, 31 = 31$
9. $x = 26, 26 - 22 = 4, 4 = 4$
10. $x = 24, 16 + 24 = 40, 40 = 40$

**Test 92—Page 96**
1. $2 \times 10 = 20$
2. $10 \div 2 = 5$
3. $8 + 10 = 18$
4. $10 - 9 = 1$
5. $4 \times 9 = 36$
6. $9 + 10 = 19$
7. $9 \times 8 = 72$
8. $9 - 7 = 2$
9. $5 + 9 = 14$
10. $9 \div 3 = 3$

**Test 93—Page 97**
1. $B = 60$
2. $Y = 12$
3. $A = 54$
4. $(6 \times 30) - (5 \times 7) = 145$
5. $(15 + 9) \times 3 \div 8 = 9$
6. $4^2 + (8 \times 7) = 72$
7. 10.5, 2.1
8. 1.7, 6.5
9. 9.8, 15.1
10. 6, 4.8

**Test 94—Page 98**
1. $V = 90$
2. $M = 8$
3. $K = 17.6$
4. $F = 6$
5. $T = 27$
6. $E = 6$
7. $Z = 35$
8. $\$66.50 \div 5 = G, G = \$13.30$
9. $G + 4 + 6 = 13, G = 3$
10. $60 \div (4 \times 3) = G, G = 5$

**Test 95—Page 99**
1. $x - 10$
2. $4x + 5y$
3. $\dfrac{(6 + x)}{10}$ or $(6 + x) \div 10$
4. four times $y$
5. two times $y$ minus five
6. $4y$
7. $3n - 5$
8. $3r$
9. $x + 1$
10. $-2x + 3y$ or $3y - 2x$

**Test 96—Page 100**
1. 48
2. 46
3. 7
4. -10

5. 21
6. 42
7. 15°C
8. $y = 80$
9. $a = 42$
10. $a = -125$

**Test 97—Page 101**
1. $a = 8$
2. $z = 9$
3. $d = 3$
4. $x = 1$
5. $x = 1$
6. $x = 2$
7. $x = 3$
8. $x = 4$
9. $a = 2$
10. $r = 5$

**Test 98—Page 102**
1. $x = 3$
2. $x = 39$
3. $b = 2$
4. $x = 20$
5. $x = -5$
6. $x = -16$
7. $y = b - c - d$
8. $x = r + c$
9. $a = n - b$
10. $x = b/d$ or $x = b \div d$

**Test 99—Page 103**
1. (-5, 0)
2. (-2, 0)
3. (0, 3)
4. (0, 7)
5. (1, 0)
6. (-5, 2)
7. (-6, -3)
8. (-3, -6)
9. (5, 5)
10. (1, -5)

**Test 100—Page 104**
1. (2, -4)
2. (4, 0)
3. (6, 4)
4. (8, 8)
5. (-2, -5)
6. (5, 2)
7. (6, 3)
8. (-6, -2)
9. (2, 2)
10. (6, 4)